Maya Angelou

These and other titles are included in The Importance Of biography series:

Alexander the Great	Adolf Hitler
Muhammad Ali	Harry Houdini
Maya Angelou	Thomas Jefferson
Louis Armstrong	Mother Jones
James Baldwin	Chief Joseph
Clara Barton	John F. Kennedy
The Beatles	Martin Luther King Jr.
Napoleon Bonaparte	Joe Louis
Julius Caesar	Douglas MacArthur
Rachel Carson	Malcolm X
Charlie Chaplin	Thurgood Marshall
Charlemagne	Margaret Mead
Cesar Chavez	Golda Meir
Winston Churchill	Michelangelo
Cleopatra	Wolfgang Amadeus Mozart
Christopher Columbus	John Muir
Hernando Cortes	Sir Isaac Newton
Marie Curie	Richard M. Nixon
Charles Dickens	Georgia O'Keeffe
Emily Dickinson	Louis Pasteur
Amelia Earhart	Pablo Picasso
Thomas Edison	Elvis Presley
Albert Einstein	Jackie Robinson
Duke Ellington	Norman Rockwell
F. Scott Fitzgerald	Eleanor Roosevelt
Dian Fossey	Anwar Sadat
Anne Frank	Margaret Sanger
Benjamin Franklin	Oskar Schindler
Galileo Galilei	William Shakespeare
Emma Goldman	John Steinbeck
Jane Goodall	Tecumseh
Martha Graham	Jim Thorpe
Lorraine Hansberry	Mark Twain
Stephen Hawking	Queen Victoria
Ernest Hemingway	Pancho Villa
Jim Henson	H. G. Wells

THE IMPORTANCE OF

Maya Angelou

by Terrasita A. Cuffie

Lucent Books, P.O. Box 289011, San Diego, CA 92198-9011

Library of Congress Cataloging-in-Publication Data

Cuffie, Terrasita A., 1964–
    Maya Angelou / by Terrasita A. Cuffie.
      p.   cm.—(The importance of)
    Includes bibliographical references (p.   ) and index.
    Summary: Discusses the life and work of the well-known
writer, entertainer, and political activist, Maya Angelou.
    ISBN 1-56006-532-X (lib. bdg. : alk. paper)
    1. Angelou, Maya—Juvenile literature.   2. Women authors,
American—20th century—Biography Juvenile literature.
3. Afro-American women civil rights workers—Biography
Juvenile literature.   4. Women entertainers—United
States—Biography Juvenile literature.   5. Afro-American
women authors—Biography Juvenile literature. [1. Angelou,
Maya. 2. Authors, American. 3. Afro-Americans Biography.
4. Women Biography.]   I. Title.   II. Series.
PS3551.N464Z6   1999
818'.5409—dc21   99–20045
[B]   CIP

Copyright 1999 by Lucent Books, Inc., P.O. Box 289011,
San Diego, California, 92198-9011

Printed in the U.S.A.

Contents

Foreword

THE IMPORTANCE OF biography series deals with individuals who have made a unique contribution to history. The editors of the series have deliberately chosen to cast a wide net and include people from all fields of endeavor. Individuals from politics, music, art, literature, philosophy, science, sports, and religion are all represented. In addition, the editors did not restrict the series to individuals whose accomplishments have helped change the course of history. Of necessity, this criterion would have eliminated many whose contribution was great, though limited. Charles Darwin, for example, was responsible for radically altering the scientific view of the natural history of the world. His achievements continue to impact the study of science today. Others, such as Chief Joseph of the Nez Percé, played a pivotal role in the history of their own people. While Joseph's influence does not extend much beyond the Nez Percé, his nonviolent resistance to white expansion and his continuing role in protecting his tribe and his homeland remain an inspiration to all.

These biographies are more than factual chronicles. Each volume attempts to emphasize an individual's contributions both in his or her own time and for posterity. For example, the voyages of Christopher Columbus opened the way to European colonization of the New World. Unquestionably, his encounter with the New World brought monumental changes to both Europe and the Americas in his day. Today, however, the broader impact of Columbus's voyages is being critically scrutinized. *Christopher Columbus,* as well as every biography in The Importance Of series, includes and evaluates the most recent scholarship available on each subject.

Each author includes a wide variety of primary and secondary source quotations to document and substantiate his or her work. All quotes are footnoted to show readers exactly how and where biographers derive their information, as well as provide stepping-stones to further research. These quotations enliven the text by giving readers eyewitness views of the life and times of each individual covered in The Importance Of series.

Finally, each volume is enhanced by photographs, bibliographies, chronologies, and comprehensive indexes. For both the casual reader and the student engaged in research, The Importance Of biographies will be a fascinating adventure into the lives of people who have helped shape humanity's past and present, and who will continue to shape its future.

IMPORTANT DATES IN THE LIFE OF MAYA ANGELOU

1928

Born Marguerite Ann Johnson in St. Louis, Missouri, on April 4.

1930

Angelou's parents send her and her brother, Bailey Jr., to live with the children's paternal grandmother in Stamps, Arkansas.

1940

Angelou graduates at the top of her eighth-grade class from Lafayette County Training School; Angelou and Bailey move to California to live with their mother, Vivian Baxter.

1945

Angelou graduates from Mission High School and gives birth to her son, Clyde Bailey Johnson.

1950

Angelou marries Tosh Angelos.

1952

Angelou divorces Angelos.

1954–1955

Appears in *Porgy and Bess* on a twenty-two-nation tour.

1957

Appears in off-Broadway play, *Calypso Heat Wave*, and records "Miss Calypso" for Liberty Records.

1959–1960

Appointed northern coordinator for the Southern Christian Leadership Conference.

1960

Produces and performs in *Cabaret for Freedom;* appears in Jean Genet's play *The Blacks*.

1961–1962

Works as the associate editor of the *Arab Observer* in Cairo, Egypt.

1963–1965

While living in Ghana, Angelou is the assistant administrator for the School of Music and Drama at the University of Ghana, Institute of African Studies; also works for the *Ghanaian Times* and appears in a production of Bertolt Brecht's *Mother Courage*.

1966–1967

Appears in *Medea* in Hollywood; writes *The Clawing Within* and *Adjoa Amissah*.

1968

Narrates "Black! Blues! Black!" a ten-part television series.

1969

Records *The Poetry of Maya Angelou* for GWP Records.

1970

Publishes *I Know Why the Caged Bird Sings* and is appointed writer in residence at the University of Kansas; chosen as a Yale University fellow.

1971

Publishes *Just Give Me a Cool Drink of Water 'Fore I Diiie*.

1972

Writes screenplay *Georgia, Georgia*.

1973

Acts in *Look Away;* marries Paul De Feu.

1974

Writes screenplay *All Day Long;* adapts Sophocles' *Ajax;* publishes *Gather Together in My Name*.

1975

Appointed to President Gerald R. Ford's American Revolution Bicentennial Council; publishes *Oh Pray My Wings Are Gonna Fit Me Well;* selected as a Rockefeller Foundation scholar in residence; receives honorary degrees from Smith College and Mills College; records *An Evening with Maya Angelou;* appointed to the board of trustees of the American Film Institute.

1976

Publishes *Singin' and Swingin' and Gettin' Merry like Christmas; Ladies' Home Journal* names her its Woman of the Year; receives an honorary doctorate from Lawrence University; writes play *And Still I Rise.*

1977

President Jimmy Carter appoints Angelou to the National Commission on the Observance of International Women's Year; receives an Emmy nomination for her role as Nyo Boto in the television miniseries *Roots;* receives the Golden Eagle award for her documentary series.

1978

Publishes her third volume of poetry, *And Still I Rise.*

1981

Publishes *The Heart of a Woman.*

1982

Receives lifetime appointment as Z. Smith Reynolds Professor of American Studies at Wake Forest University, Winston-Salem; writes television screenplay *Sister, Sister.*

1983

Publishes *Shaker, Why Don't You Sing?*

1986

Publishes *All God's Children Need Traveling Shoes.*

1987

Publishes *Now Sheba Sings the Song.*

1990

Writes screenplay for *The Women of Brewster Place* television series premiere.

1992

Publishes *I Shall Not Be Moved;* named Woman of the Year by *Essence* magazine and Distinguished Woman of North Carolina; receives Horatio Alger Award; mother, Vivian Baxter, dies.

1993

President Bill Clinton appoints Angelou the inaugural poet and she reads her poem "On the Pulse of Morning" during the inauguration ceremony; publishes *On the Pulse of Morning, Lessons in Living,* and *Wouldn't Take Nothing for My Journey Now.*

1994

Receives Grammy Award for best spoken word or nontraditional album for recording of *On the Pulse of Morning;* publishes children's poetry, *Soul Looks Back in Wonder* and *My Painted House, My Friendly Chicken, and Me.*

1995

Publishes *A Brave and Startling Truth.*

1997

Publishes *Even the Stars Look Lonesome.*

1998

Directs *Down in the Delta* for Miramax Films.

Introduction

Maya Angelou: America's Spiritual Adviser

Poet laureate, best-selling and award-winning author, and respected educator Maya Angelou has played many roles throughout her lifetime. Whether working as a cook, calypso singer, dancer, streetcar conductor, songwriter, screenwriter, journalist, wife, or mother, Angelou has always aimed high. Born in a society that sought to define and limit her aspirations, at a very young age Angelou decided to "invent" her own life and refused to succumb to society's definition of what she could become as a result of limitations placed on her race and gender.

Angelou's ability to defy obstacles such as youth, inexperience, racism, poverty, childhood molestation, sexism, naivete, and teenage motherhood has made her a much-sought-after inspirational speaker and educator. She survived these obstacles in part by maintaining a sense of hope that she could overcome them. Angelou believes that the importance of the events in her life lies in what she and others can learn from them:

> One of the first things that a young person must internalize, deep down in the blood and bones, is the understanding that although he encounters defeats, he must not be defeated. If life

teaches us anything, it may be that it's necessary to suffer some defeats. Look at the diamond: It is the result of extreme pressure. Less pressure, it is crystal; less than that, it's coal; and less than that, it is fossilized leaves or just plain dirt. It's necessary, therefore, to

Maya Angelou's resilience and determination have made her a powerful and inspirational literary figure and educator.

be tough enough to bite the bullet as it is shot into one's mouth, to bite it and stop it before it tears a hole in one's throat. One must learn to care for oneself first, so that one can then dare to care for someone else. That's what it takes to make the caged bird sing.[1]

At age seventy Angelou resides in a red-brick, colonial-style house in Winston-Salem, North Carolina, and continues to thrive as a writer and educator. She has a lifetime appointment as the Z. Smith Reynolds Professor of American Studies at Wake Forest University in Winston-Salem. She has authored five autobiographical works, six volumes of poetry, and two collections of essays, which have graced the *New York Times* best-seller lists and received critical acclaim. Her television and film credits are numerous, as are the professional and academic honors she has received. In discussing her successes, Angelou

is emphatic that her talent is not extraordinary or innate, but a result of her unrelenting self-discipline and devotion to honing her craft. She insists that "every human being is born with talent," and that talent is like "electricity" that "anyone can plug into. It's a question of whether it's used positively or negatively."[2]

Although Angelou's writing reflects her race, it remains, Angelou believes, that all people share more similarities than differences and depend on one another for moral and physical survival:

I write about the black experience, because it's what I know. But I'm always talking about the human condition, what human beings feel and how we feel. Given these circumstances, a human being will react this way: he'll be happy, will weep, will celebrate, will fall. So my books are popular in Asia, in Africa, in Europe.

In addition to her literary and academic credits, Angelou has also received acclaim for her film and television productions. In 1998 she directed the powerful feature film Down in the Delta.

Why would I, a black girl in the South, fall in love with Tolstoy or Dickens? I was Danton and Madame Defarge and all those people in A Tale of Two Cities. I was Daphne du Maurier and the Brontë sisters in a town where blacks were not allowed to cross the street. I was educated by those writers. Not about themselves and their people, but about me, what I could hope for.[3]

That sense of hope and unity and the indefatigable spirit that humans can attain have been prevalent throughout Angelou's life. It is this theme, the triumph over adversity, that fills Angelou's life and work:

I believe all things are possible for a human being, and I don't think there's anything in the world I can't do. Of course, I can't be five feet four because I'm six feet tall. I can't be a man because I'm a woman. The physical gifts are given to me, just like having two arms is a gift. In my creative source, whatever that is, I don't see why I can't sculpt. Why shouldn't I? Human beings sculpt. I'm a human being. I refuse to indulge any man-made differences between myself and another human being. I will not do it. I'm not going to live very long. If I live another fifty years, it's not very long. So I should indulge somebody else's prejudice at their whim and not for my own convenience! Never happen! Not me![4]

It is part of the human condition to suffer injustices and obstacles, and Angelou's message, that each of us can still triumph, and, yes, find joy, is an important and timeless one.

1 Growing Up Black, Southern, and Female

When Maya Angelou was a child, black Americans were systematically excluded from equal participation in society. Although the Emancipation Proclamation had abolished slavery in 1863, southern whites had preserved a political and social structure that perpetuated black inequality. In 1865 most southern states enacted a series of laws referred to as Black Codes. The Black Codes generally restricted blacks' ability to own land and access to certain skilled labor trades and even made it possible for black children to become indentured servants to whites if they were orphaned or their parents couldn't pay their debts. Many southern states also prohibited blacks and whites from marrying each other and a series of statutes commonly referred to as Jim Crow laws disenfranchised blacks by requiring them to pass literacy tests, own land, or pay poll taxes before they could vote in an election.

The federal government also sanctioned certain forms of racial discrimination, backed by the Supreme Court in its landmark 1896 decision *Plessy v. Ferguson,* which upheld state laws that established "separate but equal" public facilities. Thus, during Angelou's childhood, blacks were barred from using the public restrooms, water fountains, or parks used by whites. Furthermore, blacks were prevented from living in the same neighborhoods, attending the same schools and churches, and sitting in the same sections on public buses and railroad cars.

Marguerite Ann Johnson was born on April 4, 1928, in St. Louis, Missouri. Her brother, Bailey, one year older, was responsible for her nickname, "Maya." When he was two years old, he referred to her as "My." Both children were separated from their parents, Bailey Johnson and Vivian Baxter Johnson, when they were quite small. The couple divorced when Maya was three years old and the couple sent the children to live with their father's mother, Annie Henderson, in Stamps, Arkansas. The two children would always remember the experience, as they traveled alone, wearing tags attached to their wrists that gave their names, point of origin, and destination. Except for one short period of time, Maya and Bailey remained in Stamps, Arkansas, with their grandmother and Uncle Willie for the next ten years.

Stamps, Arkansas, was a typical small, southern rural American town during the first half of the twentieth century. Angelou describes Stamps as a town where blacks and whites lived in completely segregated communities clearly divided by a set of "railroad tracks, the swift Red River, and racial prejudice. Whites lived on the town's small rise while blacks occupied the part of town that had been known as the 'Quarters' since slavery."[5]

Throughout her childhood Angelou struggled with feelings of displacement due to her early separation from her parents. Moreover, growing up in the South took an exacting toll on her self-esteem as she struggled with racism's implicit message that a southern, black female was inferior and had very little control over her own destiny. As a child, Angelou's keen awareness of the racial divisions and the disadvantages of being black greatly affected how she measured her own self-worth. During a church Easter service, she daydreamed about what it would be like to awaken from what she perceived as an ugly dream where she was "a too-big Negro girl, with nappy black hair, broad feet and a space between her teeth that would hold a number-two pencil" transformed into one of those "sweet little white girls who were everybody's dream of what was right with the world."[6] Angelou later recalled in her book *I Know Why the Caged Bird Sings*:

> If growing up is painful for the Southern Black Girl being aware of her displacement is the rust on the razor that threatens the throat. It is an unnecessary insult. . . .
>
> The Black female is assaulted in her tender years by all those common forces of nature at the same time that she is caught in the tripartite crossfire of masculine prejudice, white illogical hate and Black lack of power.[7]

A traveling serviceman reads a sign pointing the way to the "colored" waiting room. During the early- to middle-twentieth century, segregation was common throughout America, particularly in the South.

Their grandmother created a strict and sheltered upbringing for Maya and Bailey, whose activities revolved around the activities of their grandmother's store, school, and church. Annie Henderson had accomplished much. In addition to being the proud sole proprietor of the William Johnson General Merchandise Store, or "the Store" as it was commonly called, she owned land and houses, which she rented out to poor whites.

Annie Henderson was a realist and deeply religious, locally considered the "mother of the church," and she and the children attended activities every night. On Monday evenings, Maya and Bailey accompanied their grandmother to Usher Board meeting. On Tuesdays, the mothers of the church met. Wednesdays they all attended prayer meeting. On Thursdays, the deacons met. Fridays and Saturdays were spent in preparation for Sunday, when Maya and Bailey spent a minimum of six hours in a pew under their grandmother's watchful eye.

School was also a rigid ritual governed by Maya and Bailey's grandmother and Uncle Willie. The children attended grade school at the Lafayette County Training School. Angelou described the school as a complex of two buildings which housed the grade school and the high school and sat on a dirt hill. Unlike Central School, the high school that whites attended, Lafayette County Training School didn't have expansive lush green lawns or hedges, tennis courts, or climbing ivy. The recreational equipment was limited to rusty hoops on swaying poles on a field to the left of the school that doubled as a baseball diamond and basketball court.

After school, Uncle Willie presided over each homework session with little tolerance for repeated mistakes or hesitations. After they finished their homework, Maya and Bailey were free to play with other children.

The children were close, with Bailey usually sticking up for his shier sister, whom he worshiped. Whether in response to an unkind remark about her physical appearance or teasing by her playmates about her lighter complexion or towering height, Bailey always rose to defend her. When speaking of Bailey in *Caged Bird*, Angelou writes:

> Of all the needs (there are none imaginary) a lonely child has, the one that must be satisfied, if there is going to be hope and a hope of wholeness, is the unshaking need for an unshakable God. My pretty Black brother was my Kingdom Come.[8]

Thus, Annie Henderson's and her grandchildren's world was defined by "work, duty, religion."[9] The family lived in the rear of the store and each morning Annie rose at 4:00 A.M. to begin her day's work. After a prayer thanking God for living one more day and asking for help in bridling her tongue, she would awaken Maya and Bailey. She raised Maya and Bailey to follow the same paths in life that other blacks before them had followed. The most important lesson for a black child growing up in the South was that blacks must exercise extreme caution when speaking either directly to whites or in their presence.

Blacks lived in constant fear of offending any white because of the threat of retaliation from the local Ku Klux Klan. Klan members routinely terrorized and even lynched anyone who opposed white supremacy or violated the organization's principles governing the relationship between

The Store

When asked to recall her childhood in an interview with Jeffrey M. Elliot for Sepia Magazine *in October 1977, Angelou stated that the first picture that flashed in her mind was the Store.*

"It was a glorious place. I remember the wonderful smells; the aroma of the pickle barrel, the bulging sacks of corn, the luscious, ripe fruit. You could pick up a can of snuff from North Carolina, a box of matches from Ohio, a yard of ribbon from New York. Customers could find food staples, a good variety of colored thread, mash for hogs, corn for chickens, coal oil for lamps, light bulbs for the wealthy, shoestrings, hair dressing, balloons, and flower seeds."

In Caged Bird, *Angelou characterizes the Store as her favorite place until she left Stamps at the age of thirteen.*

"Alone and empty in the mornings, it looked like an unopened present from a stranger. Opening the front doors was pulling the ribbon off the unexpected gift. The light would come in softly (we faced north), easing itself over the shelves of mackerel, salmon, tobacco, thread. It fell flat on the big vat of lard and by noontime during the summer, the grease had softened to a thick soup.

Whenever I walked into the Store in the afternoon, I sensed that it was tired. I alone could hear the slow pulse of its job half done. But just before bedtime, after numerous people had walked in and out, had argued over their bills, or joked about their neighbors, or just dropped in to give Sister Henderson a 'Hi y'all,' the promise of magic mornings returned to the Store and spread itself over the family in washed life waves."

Maya Angelou, posing with a copy of her book I Know Why the Caged Bird Sings, *has fond memories of her grandmother's general store in the small town of Stamps, Arkansas.*

blacks and whites. Angelou vividly recalls that her own family was threatened by such a raid. The local sheriff arrived on his horse to warn them that the Ku Klux Klan would ride that evening in search of a black man who supposedly had spoken unkindly to a white woman. Every black man, thus, was in danger. Grandmother Henderson took action to hide her handicapped son, Willie.

> Immediately, while the horse's hoofs were still loudly thudding the ground, Momma blew out the coal-oil lamps. She had a quiet, hard talk with Uncle Willie and called Bailey and me into the Store.
>
> We were told to take the potatoes and onions out of their bins and knock out

Notorious for their supremacist ideals and brutal violence, members of the Ku Klux Klan struck fear in the hearts of southern blacks.

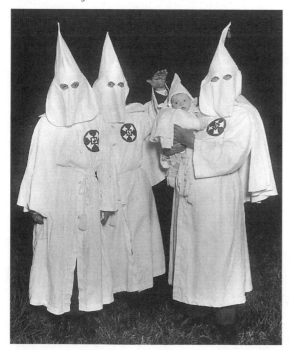

the dividing walls that kept them apart. Then with a tedious and fearful slowness Uncle Willie gave me his rubber tipped cane and bent down to get into the now-enlarged empty bin. It took forever before he lay down flat, and then we covered him with potatoes and onions, layer upon layer, like a casserole. Grandmother knelt praying in the darkened store.

It was fortunate that the "boys" didn't ride into our yard that evening and insist that Momma open the Store. They would have surely found Uncle Willie and just as surely lynched him. He moaned the whole night through as if he had, in fact, been guilty of some heinous crime. The heavy sounds pushed their way up out of the blanket of vegetables and I pictured his mouth pulling down on the right side and his saliva flowing into the eyes of new potatoes and waiting there like dew drops for the warmth of morning.[10]

Trauma in St. Louis

Except for a couple of presents sent to them one Christmas, Maya and Bailey had no contact with their mother and father and no clear memories of them. Then, without notice, Maya's father, Bailey Johnson Sr., returned to Stamps in 1935, when she was seven years old. After a short visit with his mother and old friends, Johnson collected Maya, Bailey Jr., and their belongings and returned the children to their mother in St. Louis, Missouri. It had been over four years since the children had seen their parents. Bailey was excited, and looked forward to the trip as a great joyous adventure. Maya had an entirely different feeling. Both children had discussed feeling unloved and unwanted by their parents, shipped to Stamps at such a young age. However, upon meeting their mother, Bailey fell instantly in love with her and Maya immediately felt she knew why her parents had sent them away. No one else's mother was as beautiful as Vivian Baxter. Maya reasoned that her mother was simply too beautiful to have children.

St. Louis was foreign and unsettling for Maya. The loud noises of the big city (flushing toilets, cars, trains, buses, doorbells) and such novelties as packaged foods disconcerted her. She consoled herself by escaping into the faraway places and people's lives in the Horatio Alger novels she devoured.

The move to St. Louis was traumatizing in other ways for the children. Bailey stuttered and Maya often awoke at night screaming from horrifying nightmares.

Initially, the children lived in a household that included their mother; maternal grandmother, "Grandmother Baxter"; and two uncles. Maya and Bailey seldom saw their mother except on visits to the tavern where she worked. During the year they were in St. Louis, Maya and Bailey attended Toussaint L'Ouverture Grammar School.

Mr. Freeman

After six months, their mother moved Maya and Bailey into a house she shared with her boyfriend, Mr. Freeman. While Vivian earned extra money dealing cards in a casino at night, the children stayed with Freeman.

One day when her mother hadn't returned home from work the night before and after Freeman ordered Bailey to leave the house, he raped Maya. He swore her to secrecy, threatening to kill her if she screamed and threatening to kill Bailey if she told anyone. Immediately afterward, he sent her to the local library. Because of the pain in her thighs and hips, walking was difficult and sitting on the "hard library seats" was impossible. After the painful walk home, she climbed into bed after hiding her "red and yellow stained"[11] underwear under the mattress.

Although Angelou does not detail the events that occurred after her rape clearly, she states that, when Vivian returned home, she discovered that Maya had a slight fever and assumed Maya had a cold. Then Vivian discovered the hidden underwear when she was changing the sheets. Apparently, although Vivian could tell the girl had been molested, she did little to pressure the girl to tell her about the perpetrator. Vivian did take her daughter to the hospital, where Bailey begged her to tell them who had raped her. After Bailey assured her that no one could harm him, she confessed to Bailey what had happened and Freeman was arrested. Only eight years old, Angelou had to testify against Freeman. Freeman was found guilty and sentenced to one year and one day in prison. However, he was released from custody before serving his sentence and soon afterward found brutally beaten to death, possibly by Maya's uncles.

The children resumed living with their mother's family after the trial. Grandmother Baxter prohibited them from speaking of Freeman, his death, or what had happened. The rape, Freeman's trial, and his death had a powerful effect on Maya. For the next five years she avoided speaking to anyone except Bailey. She feared that if she talked to anyone else, she might cause them to die because she thought her testifying had caused Freeman's death. She was too young to understand that she was not responsible for what had happened to her or to Freeman.

Recovery in Stamps

Shortly after the rape, Vivian sent the children back to Stamps, Arkansas, and the comfortable bosom of Annie Henderson. Angelou speculated that they were returned to Stamps because the Baxters could no longer endure her silence and sadness. After she was released from the hospital, the Baxter family expected Maya's prompt recovery. When her withdrawal continued, they became impatient. One relative was so impatient, he physically punished her. Although Maya continued her silence in Stamps, it did not offend her grandmother or the black townspeople. Thinking that she was "tender hearted" and maybe sensitive about leaving the big city and returning to the rural South, the townspeople, like her grandmother, respected her silence and simply accepted her.

Although she didn't try to force her to speak, Henderson was troubled by the child's silence and withdrawal, and, Angelou speculates, she probably asked her friend Bertha Flowers to speak to her. Ms. Flowers was a rarity in Stamps. She was an educated black woman with an almost regal bearing. Angelou's relationship with Flowers was the turning point of her childhood and the beginning of the healing process. Angelou describes Flowers as "the lady who threw me my first life line . . . one of few gentlewomen I have ever known and has remained throughout my life the measure of what a human being can be."[12] On a visit to the Store one day, Flowers requested that Maya assist her with her purchases and accompany her home. After captivating Maya with a recitation of a passage from Charles Dickens's *A Tale of Two Cities*, Flowers explained that "Words mean more than what is set down on paper. It takes the human voice to infuse them with the shades of deeper meaning." Flowers asked Maya to visit her regularly, and Flowers gave Maya assignments, such as reading and memorizing poems and later reciting them aloud to Flowers. The most important outcome of Maya's relationship with Flowers was that Flowers gave Maya a feeling of self-worth: "I was liked, and what a difference it made. I was respected not as Mrs. Henderson's grandchild or Bailey's sister but for just being Marguerite Johnson."[13]

Maya's slow and gradual transformation from a withdrawn mute to a speaking, active participant in her community occurred over five years. Reciting poetry provided a nonthreatening vehicle for speaking aloud and Maya gradually abandoned her shell. She became engrossed in the works of Rudyard Kipling, Edgar Allan Poe, Paul Laurence Dunbar, Langston Hughes, James Weldon Johnson, and William Shakespeare and even began writing her own poetry when she was nine years old.

With renewed self-esteem came academic success. She graduated at the top of her eighth-grade class. To celebrate, Henderson closed the Store on graduation day and Maya was queen for a day as she accepted gifts and good wishes. Bailey presented her with the most cherished gift—a soft leatherbound copy of Edgar Allan

Poe's poems. On graduation day, Maya's class joined the high school seniors in the small school's graduation exercises. Angelou watched the high schoolers and contemplated the meaning of graduation:

> The girls often held hands and no longer bothered to speak to the lower students. There was a sadness about them, as if this old world was not their home and they were bound for higher ground. The boys, on the other hand, had become more friendly, more outgoing. A decided change from the closed attitude they projected while studying for finals. Now they seemed not ready to give up the old school, the familiar paths and classrooms. Only a small percentage would be continuing on to college—one of the South's

Three boys play a game of marbles in their southern neighborhood. Racism and prejudice prohibited many talented black girls and boys from escaping the cycle of poverty and injustice.

A & M (agricultural and mechanical schools), which trained Negro youths to be carpenters, farmers, handymen, masons, maids, cooks and baby nurses. Their future rode heavily on their shoulders, and blinded them to the collective joy that had pervaded the lives of the boys and girls in the grammar school graduating class.[14]

After the national anthem and the principal's welcoming remarks, the children seated themselves and listened intently to the graduation speaker, Edward Donleavy, a political candidate from Texarkana, Arkansas.

Donleavy's speech was less than inspirational. He reiterated that blacks were not equal to whites. The proud graduating class hung their heads throughout Donleavy's speech. They were disappointed by Donleavy's reminder that their dreams of becoming lawyers, doctors, and scientists were unrealistic in a white-dominated society whose laws and social mores sought to limit blacks to such roles as maids, farmers, handymen, washerwomen, and athletes. Angelou's initial reaction to Donleavy's speech was dismay at being black and powerless; for a brief moment she rationalized that blacks would be better off dead than consigned to a status less than human. However, as her graduation class began to sing the Negro national anthem, "Lift Every Voice and Sing," graduation took on a new meaning for Angelou. The song reminded Angelou that blacks had suffered many defeats and yet survived. Angelou left the graduation exercises with a sense of hope and pride.

Early Writing

Angelou's manuscripts are included in the rare books and manuscripts collection of the Z. Smith Reynolds Library at Wake Forest University. The following is an excerpt from a school assignment that Angelou wrote at age nine.

"Such jolting, rumbling squeaking and creaking! Such ringing of cowbells as the cattle plodded along! And dust—dust so thick that your mouth was full of grit, your ears were—oh, very dirty, and your hair was powdered with the reddish Arkansas dust. The sun was hot and the sweat was streaming down your face streaking through the grime. But you were happy, for you were on a great adventure. You and your father and mother, brothers and sisters, and many of your neighbors were moving from your old home in the East. You were going to settle on some of the rich land in Arkansas. And you were going there not on a train of railroad cars—there weren't any—but in a train of covered wagons, pulled by strong oxen."

California

Following Maya's graduation, Henderson informed her grandchildren that it was time to send them to California, where their mother now lived. Although she cited Uncle Willie's and her own advancing age as the primary reason for the move, Maya suspected that the real reason was her desire to ensure the growing children's safety. Thirteen-year-old Bailey witnessed a white man laughing and joking about the discovery of a black man's bloated, castrated body floating in the river and asked, "Why do they hate us so much?"[15] Immediately following the incident, Annie Henderson began preparing the children for the journey. After several months of preparations, the children, along with their grandmother, traveled to Los Angeles, where they were met by Vivian Baxter.

After settling the children and their grandmother in an apartment, Baxter returned to San Francisco to make living arrangements for herself and the children. For six months the children lived in Los Angeles with their grandmother. Bailey Sr. visited occasionally. Then Annie returned to Stamps, and Vivian moved with her children to a house in Oakland that also housed Grandmother Baxter and two uncles. Maya and Bailey attended school during the week and also visited an area playground with basketball courts, a football field, and Ping-Pong tables. However, unlike Henderson, the Baxter family adults did not question the quality or quantity of their homework or grades. On Sundays, instead of attending church, the children went to the movies. Vivian Baxter eventually married a successful businessman, "Daddy Clidell," whom Maya later de-

scribed as the only father she would know. The entire family moved to San Francisco after Baxter married.

High School

Angelou's high school years in San Francisco were difficult. She had a hard time fitting in and her old feelings of self-doubt resurfaced. She was younger than most of her classmates because she had skipped the ninth grade in Los Angeles, and in San Francisco she entered the eleventh grade at age fifteen. The first school she attended was an all-girl institution where the girls were "faster, brasher, meaner and more prejudiced than those I had met at Lafayette County Training School."[16] Although many of the black students were originally southerners, they came from urban areas such as Dallas and Tulsa, not small, sheltered rural areas. Like some of the Mexican girls who carried knives entwined in their beehive hairdos, the seemingly invincible young black girls intimidated other black, Mexican, and white students who did not have their air of fearlessness.

Although the school had a significantly lower black student population, Maya gladly transferred to the George Washington High School. Angelou's academic success in Stamps had always been the hallmark of her self-esteem. At George Washington High School she had to face the fact that the white students were further advanced in their studies and academically more competitive. However, one teacher at the school made Maya's attendance there bearable and somewhat rewarding. Miss Kirwin was a "tall, florid, buxom lady with battleship gray hair"[17] who taught civics and current events. Like Bertha Flowers, Kirwin strengthened Maya's sense of self-worth, not by singling her out as a favorite but by treating her and her classmates as intellectual equals. Most importantly, Kirwin didn't regard racial or ethnic identity as cause for either negative or positive special treatment. Maya was simply "Miss Johnson." Kirwin's only reward for the right answer to a question was the word "Correct." After receiving a scholarship when she was fourteen, Maya attended evening classes and studied drama and dance at an adult college, the California Labor School.

On Her Own

During the summer of her fifteenth year, Maya traveled to Los Angeles to visit her father. Her father's live-in girlfriend resented Maya and the attention she received from her father. Maya attempted to reassure the woman that she had not meant to interfere in the relationship. The woman's response was to insult Maya's mother. Maya lost her temper and slapped the woman and the two fought until Maya broke away and left the house. As the woman ran from the house in her direction screaming and waving a knife, Maya realized that the woman had stabbed her. She quickly ran and locked herself in her father's car. Hearing the commotion, he came running from a neighbor's house. He took Maya to a couple's home where someone dressed her wounds. The next morning, it was apparent that Bailey Sr. intended to leave Maya with his friends for the duration of her stay. Angelou didn't call her mother because she feared that Vivian would seek revenge after seeing her wounds. Also re-

luctant to impose on her father's friends, Maya set out on her own with a few tuna sandwiches lumpy with pickles, three dollars plus a few Mexican coins, and a Band-Aid supply. After wandering for a full day, she discovered a group of homeless children in a junkyard. The children were a mix of black, white, and Mexican faces of different heights, sexes, and weights. At night they slept in cars. During the day, they searched for ways to make money. Each person deposited his or her daily earnings with the head of the commune, a tall boy named Bootsie. The commune had a loose code of conduct forbidding stealing and sleeping with the opposite sex. They readily accepted Maya into their community after she maintained that she didn't have a place to go and that she would abide by their rules. The six weeks she spent in the junkyard commune greatly influenced Maya:

> The unquestionable acceptance by my peers had dislodged the familiar insecurity. Odd that the homeless children, the silt of war frenzy, could initiate me into the brotherhood of man. After hunting down unbroken bottles with a white girl from Missouri, a Mexican girl from Los Angeles and a Black girl from Oklahoma, I was never again to sense myself so solidly outside the pale of the human race. The lack of criticism evidenced by our ad hoc community influenced me and set a tone of tolerance for my life.[18]

She returned home to San Francisco in the fall, but high school lessons, dating, and football games seemed irrelevant compared with her experience during her summer in Los Angeles. To make matters worse, Bailey moved out after he refused

Youthful Dreams

Throughout I Know Why the Caged Bird Sings *Angelou reflects on the impact of racism on her childhood. The following excerpt from the book describes how she dreamed of being a white child and ending the oppression she felt as a black southern female child.*

"As I watched Momma put ruffles on the hem and cute little tucks around the waist, I knew that once I put it on I'd look like a movie star. (It was silk and that made up for the awful color.) I was going to look like one of the sweet little white girls who were everybody's dream of what was right with the world. Hanging softly over the black Singer sewing machine, it looked like magic, and when people saw me wearing it they were going to run up to me and say, 'Marguerite (sometimes it was 'dear Marguerite'), forgive us, please, we didn't know who you were,' and I would answer generously, 'No, you couldn't have known. Of course I forgive you.'

Just thinking about it made me go around with angel's dust sprinkled over my face for days. But Easter's early morning sun had shown the dress to be a plain ugly cut-down from a white woman's once-was-purple throwaway. It was old-lady-long too, but it didn't hide my skinny legs, which had been greased with Blue Seal Vaseline and powdered with the Arkansas red clay. The age faded color made my skin look dirty like mud, and everyone in church was looking at my skinny legs.

Wouldn't they be surprised when one day I woke out of my black ugly dream, and my real hair, which was long and blond, would take the place of the kinky mass that Momma wouldn't let me straighten? My light-blue eyes were going to hypnotize them, after all the things they said about 'my daddy must of been a Chinaman' (I thought they meant made out of china, like a cup) because my eyes were so small and squinty. Then they would understand why I had never picked up a Southern accent, or spoke the common slang, and why I had to be forced to eat pigs' tails and snouts. Because I was really white and because a cruel fairy stepmother, who was understandably jealous of my beauty, had turned me into a too-big Negro girl, with nappy black hair, broad feet and a space between her teeth that could hold a number-two pencil."

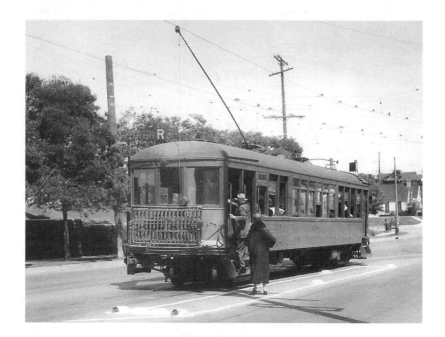

Passengers board a streetcar in San Francisco. Angelou, weary from her summer in Los Angeles and bored with her studies, quit school briefly and worked as a streetcar conductor.

to end his relationship with a white prostitute. Living at home without Bailey seemed unbearable. However, leaving home meant supporting herself, so Maya compromised and decided that she would get a job. Her mother agreed that she could get a job instead of attending school during the fall semester. After weeks of searching, she finally landed a position as a streetcar operator. After a semester of working bizarre shifts that either began or ended at dawn, Angelou quit her job and resumed her studies.

Angelou drifted through her remaining high school semesters and wrestled with a new demon, her sexuality. At sixteen, she was tall and underdeveloped compared with other girls her age. She also decided that her lack of hips or breasts, her big feet, deep voice, and skinny legs rendered her unfeminine and speculated about whether she was a "normal woman."[19] She decided that sexual intercourse would establish her as a normal woman, and matter-of-factly invited the most-sought-after boy in the neighborhood to be her partner. After intercourse, however, Maya realized that the experience had not changed her. Three weeks later she discovered that she was pregnant. She hid the pregnancy until after she attended summer school and the Mission High School in San Francisco awarded her a high school diploma. Her mother and Daddy Clidell accepted the pregnancy and her insistence that she didn't want to marry the father. A month later, in July 1945, she gave birth to her son, Clyde Bailey Johnson.

Chapter

2 Teenage Motherhood and Making a Living

In 1945, World War II ended and the country entered a period of postwar transition. Maya was seventeen, had a two-month-old son, and lived with her mother and stepfather. During the next three years, Angelou struggled with her desire to be her son's primary caretaker and the need to support him and provide him with a nuclear family. She felt tremendous guilt and remorse for having a child out of wedlock and presenting the family with another mouth to feed during hard times. In her 1974 autobiography, *Gather Together in My Name*, Angelou explains why she felt the need to strike out on her own:

> I was seventeen, very old, embarrassingly young, with a son of two months, and I still lived with my mother and stepfather.
>
> They offered me a chance to leave my baby with them and return to school. I refused. First, I reasoned with the righteous seriousness of youth, I was not Daddy Clidell Jackson's blood daughter and my child was his grandchild only as long as the union between Daddy and Mother held fast, and by then I had seen many weak links in their chain of marriage. Second, I considered that although I was Mother's child, she had left me with

others until I was thirteen and why should she feel more responsibility for my child than she had felt for her own. Those were the pieces that made up the skin of my refusal, but the core was more painful, more solid, truer. A textured guilt was my familiar, my bedmate to whom I had turned my back. My daily companion whose hand I would not hold. The Christian teaching dinned into my ears in the small town of Arkansas would not be quieted by the big-city noise.[20]

Deciding to find first employment and then a place to live, Angelou applied for a telephone operator position. She was shocked when she was informed that the company could not hire her because her scores on its applicant examination were too low. Instead, the telephone company offered her a cafeteria bus girl position and Angelou reluctantly accepted. However, humiliated that her classmates were operator trainees while she served them and cleaned their tables, she quit after one week.

Angelou often made up for her lack of experience and skills with her fierce determination to succeed and an ability to thrust herself into any role and convince others to hire her and give her an opportunity to learn. So she answered an advertisement for a Creole cook position on a Friday and spent Saturday and Sunday learning Creole cooking in preparation for her first day on Monday. Her new job paid seventy-five dollars a week. Angelou was able to rent a room with cooking privileges in a tall San Francisco Victorian house and pay an older woman to care for Clyde during the day while she worked. She was elated that she was providing for herself and her son and felt that she had finally made it.

However, Angelou constantly dreamed of a nuclear family that included a devoted husband for herself and a doting father for Clyde. She hoped that her first relationship with Curley, a kind and gentle man she met in the restaurant, would provide this. However, Curley informed Angelou that their time together was limited because he planned to join his fiancée in another state. Angelou still fantasized that he would change his mind, engrossing herself in long walks with Clyde, evening dinners,

gift exchanges, and new family life. She was devastated when reality intruded and he said good-bye. After weeks of despair and physical deterioration, her brother Bailey convinced her that a change of scene would do her good. Angelou decided to visit her father's family in Los Angeles.

Los Angeles

Angelou worked for another month to accumulate the money for her trip. Her mother didn't object to her departure, but gave her some prophetic advice that she has recalled with each endeavor throughout her life: "Be the best of anything you get into. . . . Don't chippy at anything. Anything worth having is worth working for."[21]

Despite her "wrinkled dress and cosmetic case full to reeking with dirty diapers," Angelou descended the train in the

Streetcars pass one another on a steep hill in metropolitan San Francisco. At age seventeen, Angelou struck out on her own in the big city, landing a job and renting an apartment for herself and her two-month-old son, Clyde.

Los Angeles Union Railway Terminal, "a picture of controlled dignity."[22] She mistakenly thought that her father's family would embrace her and welcome her and Clyde into the family and their home. However, after a brief hello, they admired the baby, advised her that she would need to find housing and employment, and wished her well in her travels. Angelou describes her reaction to her family's rejection:

> I was hurt because they didn't take me and my child to their bosom, and because I was a product of Hollywood upbringing and my own romanticism. On the silver screen they would have vied for me. The winner would have set me up in a cute little cottage with frangipani and roses growing in the front yard. I would always wear pretty aprons and my son would play in the Little League. My husband would come home (he looked like Curley) and smoke his pipe in the den as I made cookies for the Boy Scouts meeting.
>
> I was hurt because none of this would come true. But only in part. I was also proud of them. I congratulated myself on having absolutely the meanest, coldest, craziest family in the world.[23]

Hiding her hurt feelings with steely pride, she denied their offer of money and invented a story that she intended to settle in San Diego. As her uncle drove her to the station, she plotted her revenge:

> I decided that one day I would be included in the family legend. Someday, as they sat around in the closed circle recounting the fights, and feuds, the prides and prejudices of the Baxters, my name would be among the most illustrious. I would become a hermit.

I would seal myself off from the world, just my son and I.

> I had written a juicy melodrama in which I was to be the star. Pathetic, poignant, isolated. I planned to drift out of the wings, a little girl martyr. It just so happened that life took my script away and upstaged me.[24]

San Diego

In San Diego, Angelou checked into a hotel and the woman at the front desk gave her the name of a woman nearby who cared for children. After meeting "Mother Cleo," Angelou set out to apply for the waitress position at the Hi Hat Club. She also began taking dance lessons at a local studio that catered to navy wives. Angelou worked for over a month cleaning ashtrays and serving drinks at the Hi Hat Club. Her quickness and ability to memorize her customers' orders and preferences earned her good tips. The workday started at six in the evening and ended at two in the morning. She would awake about noon, fix lunch, and play with Clyde. As a teenage mother Angelou instinctively provided food, care, and shelter. However, throughout her autobiographical works, she refers to her youthful inability to see her son as an individual. In *Gather Together in My Name*, she writes:

> He amused me. I could not and did not consider him a person. A real person. He was my baby, rather like a pretty living doll that belonged to me. I was myself too young and unformed a human being to think of him as a human being. I loved him. He was cute. He laughed a lot and gurgled and he was mine.[25]

Liberation

In "Mother and Freedom," from her 1997 collection of inspirational essays Even the Stars Look Lonesome, *Angelou recalls leaving home at age seventeen with a two-month-old son and her mother's advice to "follow what's right."*

"More than forty years have passed since Vivian Baxter liberated me and handed me over to life. During those years I have loved and lost, I have raised my son, set up a few households and walked away from many. I have taken life as my mother gave it to me on that strange graduation day all those decades ago.

In the intervening time when I have extended myself beyond my reach and come toppling Humpty-Dumpty-down on my face in full view of a scornful world, I have returned to my mother to be liberated by her one more time. To be reminded by her that although I had to compromise with life, even life had no right to beat me to the ground, to batter my teeth down my throat, to make me knuckle down and call it Uncle. My mother raised me and then freed me."

While working at the Hi Hat Club, Angelou befriended two of her customers, who she later found out were prostitutes. One evening, Angelou accepted the two women's invitation to dine in their home. Throughout the evening the two women teased and taunted Angelou. Angelou was embarrassed by their raucous physical intimacy and humor and felt pressured to accept their invitation to smoke marijuana. Humiliated by her youth and inexperience and reeling from her first experience with marijuana, Angelou decided to fabricate a worldly personal history, telling the two women that she had been a madam in another city and had to shut down her operation because of the police. Taken in, the two women's perception changed from amusement and contempt for her youth to admiration and respect. Earlier in the evening they had informed Angelou that their landlord was not going to renew their lease due to their lifestyle. Angelou proposed that the three of them enter into a business arrangement. Angelou offered to rent the house for them, act as their madam, and channel business to them from the Hi Hat Club. Although she didn't prostitute herself, Angelou was not above brokering their services for what she considered lucrative fees. The two women were skeptical at first but accepted her proposal. Only eighteen years old, she was proud of herself for gaining the upper hand and turning ridicule to apparent respect.

Angelou's life revolved around her job at the Hi Hat Club, dance lessons, raising Clyde, and haunting the library as she discovered Russian writers Fyodor Dostoyevsky, Ivan Turgenev, and Anton Chekhov.

Late at night she collected her percentage of the prostitutes' fees. Business was profitable but very risky. Angelou feared that if her secret were discovered, Mother Cleo would ask her to move out and refuse to continue caring for Clyde. Though she could afford better lodgings and virtually any child care with the savings she was secretly accumulating, Angelou had grown fond of Mother Cleo and her family and cared about their opinion of her. She had even joined Mother Cleo's church. Their home reminded her of the stable, caring atmosphere at her grandmother's. When she examined this period in *Gather Together in My Name*, Angelou wondered at her sanity:

> Upon reflection, I marvel that no one saw through me enough to bundle me off to the nearest mental institution. The fact that it didn't happen depended less on my being a good actress than the fact that I was surrounded, as I had been all my life, by strangers. The world of waitress, dreamer, madam and mother might have continued indefinitely, except for another of life's unexpected surprises.[26]

The unexpected surprise was an argument that ensued when Angelou discovered that the two women were not disclosing all their income. Unable to resolve the dispute, the two women threatened to expose Angelou to the police. Suddenly what had been a frivolous scheme to gain the two women's respect involved a real prospect of arrest and prosecution. Angelou quickly decided to abandon her scheme. She realized that if she were sentenced to jail, she could be declared an unfit mother and lose Clyde, depriving him of the life she desperately wanted for him. Angelou abandoned her shiny new car, rushed with Clyde to the train station, and boarded a train bound for Stamps and the protective and courageous arms of Annie Henderson and the "shield of anonymity" she had known as a child.

Stamps, Arkansas, Revisited

By returning to Stamps, Angelou moved against the tide of black migration. During World War II, southern youths, both black and white, had moved to the North to take jobs in factories. After the war few blacks returned to the barren South and its racial terrors. However, to Angelou, the South was home. Seeing the Store and its warm kitchen brought tears to her eyes and seemed to erase the hurt of San Francisco, San Diego, and unsuccessful romantic relationships.

However, Angelou's return lasted only eight days. After five years in California, attending schools with whites, living and working alongside whites, she was not prepared to resume an attitude of deference and subservience required of southern blacks. As a child, she rarely saw whites and was not directly subjected to racist behavior. However, as an adult black woman she was no longer insulated by that anonymity. An outsider among her peers, Angelou turned to white Stamps, desperate for recognition and respect and spoiling for a fight. Dressed in pumps and gloves, Angelou descended on the general merchandise store in white Stamps. She refused to take orders from a white store employee and even threatened to slap her if she didn't treat her with the respect that she deserved. Annie Henderson was waiting on the steps when she arrived home. Someone had called her from the general merchandise store and informed her of her granddaughter's actions. Slapping her into reality, she reminded Angelou that her years in California did not immunize her from the possibility of violent assault or murder, and her defiance put the entire black community at risk of white violence. Believing nothing could protect her and the family except the Lord and some miles, Henderson packed Angelou's and the baby's things and arranged for someone to take them to Louisville. Angelou's grandmother and Uncle Willie stood in the road crying and waving as the wagon headed for the train station.

San Francisco and Escapism

Vivian welcomed Angelou and Clyde into her fourteen-room home in San Francisco as if they had been away on a extended vacation. Angelou's former classmates were a world apart, attending college while she worked at low-paying, low-skilled jobs in restaurant kitchens. She longed for professional work and intellectual stimulation. Angelou decided that she could improve her and her son's life by joining the army. Her visions of tailored skirts and sweaters accented with dainty gloves and a suburban house surrounded by a white picket fence were dashed, however, when an army clerk informed her that her attendance at the California Labor School rendered her a card-carrying Communist and unfit for military service. Angelou had had no idea that the army considered the California Labor School a Communist organization,

and she had denied participation in Communist activities or organizations on her army application. The army declined to prosecute her for falsifying her application, but she was not considered for induction. Smoking marijuana eased the pain and Angelou took a job as a restaurant swing-shift waitress. She "learned new postures" and "developed new dreams, and saw life as an amusement." Wafting on the "long slow drag of the narcotic," Angelou dreamed of the handsome man that would save her and "love her to distraction."[27]

R. L. Poole appeared on her doorstep unannounced after a record store employee told him that Angelou constantly talked about dancing, and told her that he needed a dance partner. Having been a cook, waitress, streetcar conductor, bus girl, and madam, she thought, why not a dancer? Besides, Angelou felt that she was better prepared to be a dancer than any of her previous roles. She had actually studied dance. Soon Angelou could see that Poole was skeptical, however, when she revealed that she had not studied jazz or tap. Quickly she assured him that she had won various dance contests and could do the jitterbug, Texas hop, off time, boogie-woogie, camel walk, and split. Worried that he was losing interest, she stood up to demonstrate her split, but, out of practice, she came to a sudden stop two inches from the floor, horrified that her impromptu audition had left her with a torn skirt, pain rippling through her thighs, one foot lodged beside the leg of her mother's heavy oak table and the other slammed into the gas heater pipe. Stubborn pride made her refuse Mr. Poole's outstretched hand and offer to help. However, in attempting to extricate herself she broke the gas pipe and leaking fuel began to hiss.

Angelou began moonlighting as a dancer in San Francisco. Despite her love of performing, her short-lived dance career ended when Poole reconciled with his girlfriend and former dance partner.

Poole fixed the gas leak; Angelou, certain he would make his own escape, rolled over on the floor and cried. Instead, Poole complimented her legs and hired her.

Dreaming of dancing on Broadway, Angelou eventually quit her job at the restaurant so that she could spend her time studying dance and dancing with Poole. Her mother helped her financially. Once she conquered her initial stage fright, Angelou loved the glow of the lights and mostly drunken audiences' reverence for her dancing. Though Angelou and Poole rehearsed diligently, their engagements were limited to a few one-night jobs in convention halls and Elks events. The couple

soon became romantically involved, but, with the return of Poole's former dance partner and girlfriend, Angelou's career and relationship with Poole ended.

In need of work and some distance from Poole's rejection, Angelou decided to settle in Stockton, California, eighty miles away, where a friend of Vivian Baxter's offered Angelou a job as a restaurant fry cook. Stockton promised a new life, but Angelou missed the bright lights, music, and beckoning audiences. To accommodate her work schedule, Angelou arranged for Clyde to live with the neighborhood's surrogate mother, Big Mary, six days a week, and spent her day off with her son.

Although Angelou yearned for the idealized lifestyles she saw in movies and magazines, she would continue to face hardships in her life.

Yet she continued to fantasize about a *Good Housekeeping* lifestyle, complete with a doting husband and house with the proverbial white picket fence. Then Angelou met gambler and married man Louis David Tolbrook at the restaurant.

Angelou wanted to please and was by nature eager to meet others' expectations. She believed Tolbrook's tales of mistreatment by his wife and was devasted when he informed her that he would have to leave town to escape underworld killers after him for over five thousand dollars in gambling debts. She quickly agreed to Tolbrook's suggestion that she work as a prostitute in a house to help him pay his debts so that

they could eventually be together. Angelou could not see that she was one of many women who worked for Tolbrook in various brothels around the city and that he had no intention of leaving his wife and setting up housekeeping with her and Clyde.

Fortunately, fate intervened when Angelou received word that her mother was ill and needed her in San Francisco. Leaving Clyde with Big Mary, she went home to find her mother hospitalized following an emergency hysterectomy and Bailey consumed with despair over the sudden death of his fiancée. She was further troubled by Bailey's increasing dependence on heroin and his rejection of her help to break his habit. During a heated argument in which Bailey ridiculed her jobs slinging hash, a stung Angelou blurted out that she was working in a house as a prostitute to help Tolbrook so they could marry. Incensed by her naivete, Bailey demanded that she go to Stockton, end the relationship with Tolbrook, and return home with Clyde. Fearing Bailey's retaliation against Tolbrook, Angelou decided to pacify him by complying with his demands but intended to resume her relationship with Tolbrook when Bailey calmed down.

However, when she arrived in Stockton, Angelou discovered that Clyde's caretaker, Big Mary, had kidnapped him and left town. Angelou immediately drove to Tolbrook's house to seek his help in finding Clyde. She was unprepared for the angry encounter that followed; Tolbrook was furious with her for appearing at the home where he lived with his wife. He demanded that she leave immediately and never addressed the issue of Clyde's kidnapping. Angelou, suddenly aware of her stupidity, had no time for self-pity. She had to find her son.

Angelou traced Big Mary to a farm in Bakersfield and she immediately made her way there by bus. After several inquiries she was led to a seemingly deserted farm. Angelou spotted three-year-old Clyde standing in a field. Clutching him in her arms, nineteen-year-old Angelou understood for the first time that Clyde was a unique and separate person with his own needs, not a "beautiful appendage of herself."[28]

Back in San Francisco, Angelou moved in with her mother and took another job cooking in a restaurant. Cain, the restaurant owner, also paid Angelou to design a new menu, but when it became clear that patrons didn't appreciate the changes, Cain returned to the old menu and hired Angelou as his chauffeur. Cain also managed boxers, so Angelou was exposed to professional boxing and the brutality of

Life 201

In a 1974 interview for Playgirl, *Angelou and Stephanie Caruana discussed the naivete and pain of Angelou's years in San Francisco. Expressing no bitterness, Angelou explained the lessons of that experience and her formula for survival.*

"Well, I say, representing some inscrutable and nonsensical Fate, we call this course *Life 201*. Ready! Okay. Yep! And the scars that you can't help but acquire can be truly marks of beauty, like dimples or a cleft chin. You decide: That hurt. I will not deny that hurt. But I will not carry that hurt into another circumstance where I may not be hurt. But it makes your voice a little softer. When you've just been raped, abused, or assaulted in some way in the street and you walk into a room, you have no idea what has happened to the other people in that room. . . . You have no idea what those people have to give you. Their stories might make you understand. 'Honey, you was fishing in very shallow water. There were sharks out where I was.'

Living life fully, fiercely, devotedly, makes you much more able to accept other people who are doing the same. All we're trying to do is get from birth to death. And you can't fail. Even if you only live five minutes, you have succeeded. And everybody's out there, trying to do the same thing. Some don't know it, and they think they have to step on your neck to survive. It's unfortunate for them. If I ever see someone trying to do that, I try to encourage the person who is standing underneath to move away, so that ill-informed person can gain some understanding. And I certainly move away. I am not helping anybody if I allow them to use or abuse me."

The Most Important Virtue

In 1977, Judith Rich interviewed Angelou in her home while her young grandson toddled at her feet. As Angelou busied herself in the kitchen with lunch preparations, she commented on the purpose of her autobiography, Gather Together in My Name.

"What I tried to show in *Gather Together* was, all through people were good to me. People were pretty bad to me too. But, more important, they were pretty good. Those acts of generosity that people showed me saved me a great deal.

I've always had the feeling that life loves the liver of it. You must live it and life will be good to you, give you experiences. They may not all be pleasant, but nobody promised you a rose garden. But more than likely if you dare, what you get are the marvelous returns. Courage is probably the most important of the virtues, because without courage you cannot practice any of the other virtues, you can't say against a murderous society, I oppose you murdering. You got to have courage to do so. I seem to have known that a long time and found great joy in it."

bouts in which contestants were beaten senseless and even died as crowds cheered. Personally outraged by a boxer's death at one match, she confronted Cain and stormed out. She was not surprised when Cain's letter terminating her services arrived at her home the following day. For the first time, Angelou had lost her sense of courage, strength, and belief in herself. With no plan of attack, she "sat down defenseless to await life's next assault."[29]

A week later, one of the restaurant's customers, Troubadour Martin, knocked on her door and asked her if she would work with him in selling "hot" women's clothes. All she had to do was to provide a place where women could meet in the company of other women to try on the clothes he would provide. Angelou readily agreed. After two months, she had regained her spirits, and her closets in her Oakland apartment were filled with beautiful and fashionable new suits, dresses, sweaters, and stockings. Angelou began fantasizing about becoming Mrs. Troubadour Martin despite her knowledge of Martin's serious narcotic habit. To her he was kind, quiet, and generous.

Angelou had romanticized every relationship with a man in the past and did the same with Troubadour Martin. Now, troubled by what she thought was an emotionally distant relationship, she decided that she and Troubadour could not achieve ultimate closeness until they shared the same high—heroin. She pouted and demanded that he share his hidden world with her. He complied. As they entered a hotel room filled with individuals of different races and sexes slumped against the walls in various states of consciousness, Angelou was confronted with the ugliness of drugs and addiction. The shock was intensified when Troubadour closed the bathroom door, cinched his tie around his arm, and viciously jabbed a needle in his arm searching for an exposed vein, ignoring the pain. Angelou describes the critical moment in which she chose not to enter the dangerous world of narcotic addiction in *Gather Together in My Name:*

> I thought about the kindness of the man. I had wanted him before for the security I thought he'd give me. I loved him as he slouched, nodding, his mouth open and the saliva sliding down his chin as slowly as the blood had flowed

down his arm. No one had ever cared for me so much. He had exposed himself to me to teach me a lesson and I learned it as I sat in the dark car inhaling the odors of the wharf. The life of the underworld was truly a rat race, and most of its inhabitants scurried like rodents in the sewers and gutters of the world. I had walked the precipice and seen it all; and at the critical moment, one man's generosity pushed me safely away from the edge.[30]

Angelou remembers that "I had no idea what I was going to make of my life, but I had given a promise and found my innocence. I swore I'd never lose it again."[31] Angelou thanked Troubadour for his kindness and, collecting herself and Clyde, returned to her mother's house in San Francisco.

3 Married Life and the Making of a Performer

Turning from her relationship with Troubadour Martin and the traps of narcotic addiction, Angelou and three-year-old Clyde struggled for the next two years as she juggled two jobs, in a real estate office and downtown dress shop. Angelou lived with her mother for a brief period until she found a room to rent. Her combined wages could barely pay her rent and Clyde's caretaker. Angelou describes the stress that working two jobs placed on her son's emotional development and their relationship in *Singin' and Swingin' and Gettin' Merry like Christmas:*

> For two years we had spun like water spiders in a relentless eddy. I had to be free to work for our support, but the babysitters were so expensive I had to have two jobs to pay their fees and my own rent. I boarded him out six days and five nights a week.

> On the eve of my day off, I would go to the babysitter's house. First he'd grab the hem of my dress, then wrap his arms around my legs and hold on screaming as I paid the weekly bill. I would pry his arms loose, then pick him up and walk down the street. For blocks, as I walked, he would scream. When we were far enough away, he'd relax his stranglehold on my neck and

I could put him down. We'd spend the evening in my room. He followed me every turn and didn't trust me to go to the bathroom and return. After dinner, cooked in the communal kitchen, I would read to him and allow him to try to read to me.

> The next day was always spent at the park, the zoo, the San Francisco Museum of Art, a cartoon movie house or any cheap or free place of entertainment. Then, on our second evening he would fight sleep like an old person fighting death. By morning, not quite awake, he would jerk and make hurtful noises like a wounded animal. I would still my heart and wake him. When he was dressed, we headed back to the sitter's house. He would begin to cry a few blocks from our destination. My own tears stayed in check until his screams stabbed from behind the closed doors and stuck like spearheads in my heart.[32]

Whenever Angelou found herself with the odd free hour between jobs, she headed for the Melrose Record Shop on Fillmore Boulevard and the works of jazz musicians and singers such as Charlie Parker, Billie Holliday, Sarah Vaughn, and Nat King Cole. She was baffled by the white store manager's friendly interest in her. The manager, Louise Parker, voluntarily offered to open a credit account for Angelou and sought Angelou's opinion of the store's inventory of black artists. She completely surprised Angelou by offering her a job as a sales clerk. Working at the record store would enable her to quit her evening job and spend more time with Clyde.

Angelou accepted Parker's job offer. In a 1974 interview with Stephanie Caruana, Angelou recalls the importance of her friendship with Louise Parker:

> I went to work in a record shop and began to learn about music. And I made my first white friend—the woman who owned the store. She introduced me to another way of life. With her help, I began to give up my ignorance and become aware. I'll never know what she saw in that twenty-year-old, six foot tall, closed, withdrawn black girl. But somehow she was perceptive enough to know she had something to give me.[33]

Although working one job meant more time with her son, Angelou was still dissatisfied with Clyde's development and believed he would benefit from her being a full-time mother. Again she envisioned marriage as the perfect solution, but had no prospects. She then contemplated welfare but immediately abandoned that possibility, as she explains in *Singin' and Swingin'*:

> And welfare was absolutely forbidden. My pride had been starched by a family who assumed unlimited authority in its own affairs. A grandmother, who raised me, my brother and her own two sons, owned a general merchandise store. She had begun her business in the early 1900's in Stamps, Arkansas, by selling meat pies to saw men in a lum-

While working in the Melrose Record Shop, Angelou was surrounded by the works of jazz and singing sensations such as Billie Holliday (pictured).

ber mill, then racing across town in time to feed workers in a cotton-gin mill four miles away.

My brother Bailey, who was a year older than I and seven inches shorter, had drummed in my youthful years: "You are as intelligent as I am"—we both agreed that he was a genius—"and beautiful. And you can do anything."

My beautiful mother, who ran businesses and men with autocratic power, taught me to row my own boat, paddle my own canoe, hoist my own sail. She warned, in fact, "If you want something done, do it yourself."

I hadn't asked them for help (I couldn't risk their refusal) and they loved me. There was no motive on earth which

Singin' and Swingin'

In a 1974 interview with journalist Stephanie Caruana for Playgirl, *Angelou recalls the beginning of her career as an entertainer in San Francisco.*

"I began taking more dance lessons, and eventually I got a dance scholarship that took me to New York City. Then I got a job at the Shakedown, a strip joint in the North Beach area of San Francisco. My costume consisted of two sequins and a feather.

There were three other dancers, all white, and all strippers. But I didn't strip, because I didn't have anything on to begin with. They paid me $75 a week plus what I could make on B-drinks. When men asked me to have a drink with them, I would explain that the drinks I got were only 7-Up—so the best thing would be to buy a bottle of champagne instead. I made a lot of money because I was honest about it.

I danced fifteen minutes of every hour, six times a night. The other ladies would go out and strip, and the band would play, 'Tea for Two,' or something like that, because the women weren't into what they were doing, and the band was bored with all that grind, grind, grind. But I was a *dancer*, and I loved it. . . . San Francisco started hearing about this dancer in this B-joint, and gradually nontourists, and the nonlecherous old men, started coming to see me. Then I met the people from the Purple Onion across the street.

One night Mort Sahl was playing there, with guitarist Stan Wilson. They finished their very elegant gigs and came to pick me up. We were all sitting around at someone's house, when the singer who was starring at the Purple Onion began saying how much she hated singing calypso music. I said there was some great calypso music, and I sang one song. She said, 'Oh, now I understand! You are supposed to take my place in the show, because I'm going to New York.' So I took some singing lessons from a wonderful coach, and a few weeks later, I opened at the Purple Onion—as the star.

People would line up outside for blocks, waiting to get in. In the middle of a song, I'd forget the lyrics, so I would start to dance. And they loved it."

would bring me, bowed, to beg for aid from an institution which scorned me and a government which ignored me. It had seemed that I would be locked in the two jobs and the weekly baby-sitter terror until my life was done. Now with a good salary, my son and I could move back into my mother's house.[34]

Angelou approached her mother and the two settled on a monthly payment for Angelou's rent and an arrangement for Angelou to pay the housekeeper for child care. Angelou writes that "For months, life was a pleasure ring and we walked safely in its perimeter."[35] Clyde was in school, reading well, and, encouraged by his mother, began his own love affair with books. His separation anxiety gradually dissolved.

Marriage and Good Housekeeping

Angelou characterizes her life in her early twenties as an "assemblage of strivings and my energies were directed toward acquiring more than the basic needs." She was "as much a part of the security conscious fifties as the quiet young white girls who lived their pastel Peter Pan–collared days in clean, middle-class neighborhoods." Like other young black women, Angelou dressed in "gay colors" and longed to be one man's woman. In fact, the black community was increasingly composed of unmarried women "bearing lonely pregnancies and wishing for two and one half children each who would gurgle happily behind that picket fence while we drove our men to work in our friendly-looking station wagon."[36]

Angelou met her first husband, Tosh Angelos, a sailor of Greek descent, when he was perusing the record store shelves searching for a Charlie Parker record. During subsequent visits, he engaged Angelou in long conversations. After learning that Angelou had a young son, Tosh Angelos asked if he could escort them to the park on Angelou's day off from work. Angelou accepted the invitation with reservations. After all, the husband she dreamed of daily was six feet, three inches and black, not two inches shorter than she and white. Despite her misgivings, Angelou set a date for an outing to Golden Gate Park. Tosh and Clyde immediately became friends, playing handball and chess and enjoying a picnic lunch. The day ended at Angelou's house, where Maya introduced Tosh to her mother.

Barely civil, Vivian questioned Tosh Angelos regarding his intentions. She specifically wanted to know where he was from, where he had met her daughter, and where he intended to live. After his departure and Angelou's reminder that her mother and brother Bailey also had white acquaintances, Vivian Baxter cautioned her daughter, "They are friends. And That's All. There's a world of difference between laughing together and loving together."[37] Angelou nevertheless agreed to let Tosh take Clyde on excursions alone, aware that Tosh was courting her through her son.

However, she was torn between her desire for family stability and the historically troubled relationship between white and black Americans. Therefore, Angelou pretended that she was unaware of Tosh's affections:

I couldn't let him know I knew. The knowledge had to remain inside me, unrevealed, or I would have to make a decision, and that decision had been made for me by the centuries of slavery, the violation of my people, the violence of whites. Anger and guilt decided before my birth that Black was Black and White was White and although the two might share sex, they must never exchange love. . . . I would never forget the slavery tales, or my Southern past where all whites, including the poor and ignorant, had the right to speak rudely to and even physically abuse any Negro they met. I knew the ugliness of white prejudice.[38]

The friendship deepened and Tosh Angelos soon proposed marriage. Vivian was livid and gravely concerned; marriage to a white man was against her beliefs, marriage to a poor white man inconceivable. Angelou summarizes her response to Vivian's challenge, "What's going to happen to you?" in *Singin' and Swingin':*

I hoped not much more than had happened already. At three years old I had been sent by train from California to Arkansas, accompanied only by my four-year-old brother; raped at seven and returned to California at thirteen. My son was born when I was sixteen, and determined to raise him I had worked as a shake dancer in night clubs, fry cook in hamburger joints, dinner cook in a Creole restaurant and once had a job in a mechanic's shop, taking the paint off cars with my hands.[39]

Vivian Baxter pressed on. She argued that Tosh Angelos's wedding gift to Angelou would be "the contempt of his people and the distrust of [her] own." Angelou countered that her gift to the proposed marriage was "a mind crammed with a volatile mixture of insecurities and stubbornness, and a five year old son who had never known a father's discipline."[40] Unable to answer her mother when asked if she loved Tosh Angelos, Angelou responded that she was marrying him simply because he asked her. Angelou invited Bailey to have dinner with her and Tosh. Bailey had dropped out of high school after the eleventh grade but continued to engross himself in literature. During the day he worked as a waiter on Southern Pacific Railroad dining cars and at night he read Aldous Huxley, Philip Wylie, and Thomas Wolfe. Bailey and Tosh found an instant common ground in discussing literature and jazz. After dinner, Bailey gave Maya a sloppy kiss on the cheek and told her to marry him if she wanted to and be happy. With Bailey's blessing and her mother's grudging acceptance, Angelou married Tosh Angelos at the local courthouse.

Duties of a Housewife

For a year the new family resided in a large flat in *Good Housekeeping* bliss. At Tosh's insistence, Angelou quit her job and spent her days perfecting her duties as a housewife, keeping a spotless house with floors dangerous from daily wax applications and furniture "slick with polish"; cooking "well-balanced meals and molding fabulous jello desserts."[41] Tosh Angelos was an attentive and appreciative husband and devoted father. However, he was an introvert; he didn't want visitors in his home and didn't understand Angelou's and Clyde's need for friends. Other than her best friend, Ivonne, Tosh believed that Angelou's old friends were intellectually inferior and not worth her time and viewed potential new friends as untrustworthy. Although Angelou ignored Tosh's refusal to allow visits from Angelou's and Clyde's friends to their home, she was troubled by her husband's angry assertion that God didn't exist. Unable to openly challenge her husband's beliefs, Angelou secretly attended Sunday church services and signed the roster with her maiden name.

Wrapped in Tosh's "cocoon of safety" Angelou didn't begin to notice the public reaction to her marriage until a year passed. Then she became aware of arm nudging, stares, and frowns when the three attended movies or visited local parks. Feeling guilty, Angelou dropped her eyes when she encountered other blacks in public. She felt that she couldn't explain to them that her husband wasn't responsible for the degradation that blacks suffered. But with Clyde's statement of his desire to have straight "good" hair like his father's and Tosh's contempt for and refusal to allow Angelou's participation in church, Angelou could no longer fantasize

that the marriage was stable. Tosh grew increasingly agitated and finally proclaimed that he was simply tired of being married. To complicate matters, Angelou was hospitalized for several weeks for complications associated with an appendectomy. While she was hospitalized, her grandmother died in Stamps. The marriage ended completely a year later. Angelou did not ask Tosh for support and the small bank account that he left them dwindled quickly. Once again, Angelou had to find employment to support herself and Clyde.

Maya, the Entertainer

Angelou responded to an advertisement, Female Dancers Wanted—Good Pay from the Garden of Allah, a dingy nightclub on a strip known as the International Settlement in San Francisco. After a brief audition, Angelou was hired. While dancing at the Garden of Allah, Angelou met a group of entertainers who would change her life.

After assuming the persona of a Cuban calypso singer, Angelou gained fame as an entertainer at the Purple Onion. Here, she poses for the cover of a record album.

They encouraged her to audition for a singing position at a basement cabaret called the Purple Onion, a step up from the Garden of Allah in patronage and talent. With the help of her new friends, which included drama coach Lloyd Clark, Angelou created a persona for her act, that of a Cuban calypso singer. Clark first decided that the name Marguerite wasn't exotic enough. So Angelou informed him that her brother had called her Maya since childhood. They readily agreed that Maya would be perfect. Deciding that Angelos was too Italian for a Cuban, they settled on

While employed at the Purple Onion, Angelou became acquainted with up-and-coming entertainers, including comedienne Phyllis Diller.

Angelou. The audition went well and the managers signed Maya Angelou to a three-month contract.

Performing as a Cuban calypso singer, Angelou became a popular entertainer. Reporters hounded her for interviews and audiences loved her. People recognized her on the street and one fan even formed a ten-member fan club. She shared billing with various entertainers including a young comedienne, Phyllis Diller.

After one evening performance Angelou was approached by George Hitchcock, a young playwright, and the two became friends. Angelou would recite Shakespearean sonnets and Paul Laurence Dunbar (an American poet) during visits to Hitchcock's home. Her friendship with Hitchcock was strictly platonic but intellectually stimulating and emotionally rewarding. Through Hitchcock, Angelou met and befriended others interested in the arts.

During this time, Angelou saw George Gershwin's modern opera *Porgy and Bess,* starring Leontyne Price and William Warfield. The play elicited an array of emotions from Angelou. She "laughed and cried, exulted and mourned." After the curtain closed, Angelou sat "stunned" in her seat wrestling with the thought that "*Porgy and Bess* had shown her the greatest array of Negro talent [she] had ever seen."[42]

Motivated by the *Porgy and Bess* performance, Angelou began composing her own calypso songs for her act and music for previously written poetry. While she was performing one night, the *Porgy and Bess* cast members visited the Purple Onion and Angelou joined them for a late supper. Several nights later, one of the show's producers came to the Purple Onion and asked her if she would like to audition for a dancing and singing role in the touring production. The audition was successful, but Angelou was forced to decline the offer due to her contract with the Purple Onion. Later, when Angelou's contract with the Purple Onion expired, the *Porgy and Bess* producers offered her the chorus role of Ruby and she quickly accepted and made arrangements for her mother to care for Clyde during her absence. She had second thoughts about leaving her young son but Ivonne reassured her that Clyde would be with family. Angelou journeyed to Montreal, where the *Porgy and Bess* ensemble rehearsed.

Porgy and Bess toured Europe for a year. Angelou was overwhelmed by the professionalism and talent of the cast. Although comfortable with the dance sequences,

Inherited Art

In her 1997 collection of essays, Even the Stars Look Lonesome, *Angelou recalls in "Art for the Sake of the Soul" a lesson she learned during her stint with* Porgy and Bess. *The sets had not arrived and the cast had to do impromptu solos.*

"I thought of a song my grandmother sang in that little town of Arkansas. Every Sunday for ten years, I had gone through the same ritual: We would gather in church. Fifteen minutes after the service began the preacher would say, 'And now we'll be privileged with a song from Sister Henderson.' Each Sunday, my grandmother would respond, 'Me?' Then she would take her time, look up at the ceiling as if she was considering: What on earth could I possibly sing? And every Sunday she sang the same song. In Morocco, all alone on the stage, I sang her song:

I'm a poor pilgrim of sorrow.
I'm lost in this wild world alone.

I sang the whole song through, and when I finished, forty-five hundred Arabs jumped up, hit the floor and started to shout. I was young and ignorant. I had no idea of the power of this, my inherited art. . . .

They had sung Respighi, Rossini, Bach, Bloch, Beethoven, lovely lieder and lovely Britten art songs, and they have been well received. And I had sung what Dr. Du Bois called a sorrow song, not written by the free and easy, not written by anyone credited with being creative, and forty-five hundred people had leaped into the palm of my hand.

Great art belongs to all people, all the time—indeed it is made for the people by the people."

Angelou had to overcome her tone deafness and inability to sight read. After rehearsals in Montreal, the company successfully performed in Italy, Paris, Yugoslavia, Russia, Egypt, Greece, Israel, Morocco, Spain, and Switzerland. While the company was touring Rome, Angelou received a disturbing letter from her mother. Vivian had returned to working nights as a dealer in a Las Vegas Negro casino, and there would be no one home to take care of Clyde. Clyde missed his mother terribly and had developed a rash that wasn't responding to medical treatment. Angelou quickly gave notice to the producers. Although sympathetic, they informed her that since she was resigning her position, they could not pay for her return ticket home, which cost over a thousand dollars. Angelou gave African dance lessons during the day and danced at nightclubs in the evening to earn the

Landing the role of Ruby in the opera Porgy and Bess, *Angelou began touring with the acting company, visiting exotic locations in Europe.*

Keeping Art Alive

"That is living art, created to encourage people to hang on, stand up, forbear, continue.

I suggest that we must be suspicious of censors who say they mean to prohibit our art for our own welfare. I suggest that we have to question their motives and tend assiduously to our own personal and national health and our general welfare. We must replace fear and chauvinism, hate, timidity and apathy, which flow in our national spinal column, with courage, sensitivity, perseverance and, I even dare say, 'love.' And by 'love' I mean that condition in the human spirit so profound it encourages us to develop courage. It is said that courage is the most important of all the virtues, because without courage you can't practice any other virtue with consistency.

We must infuse our lives with art. . . . We should have a well-supported regional theater in order to oppose regionalism and differences that keep us apart. We need nationally to support small, medium and large art museums that show us images of ourselves, those we like and those we dislike. In some way that is very important to us we need to see those we dislike even more than those we like because somehow we need at least glancing visions of how we look 'as in a mirror darkly.'

Our singers, composers and musicians must be encouraged to sing the song of struggle, the song of resistance to degradation, resistance to our humiliation, resistance to the eradication of all our values that would keep us going as a country. Our actors and sculptors and painters and writers and poets must be made to know that we appreciate them, that in fact it is their work that puts starch in our back bones.

We need art to live fully and to grow healthy. Without it we are dry husks drifting aimlessly on every ill wind, our futures are without promise and our present without grace."

money. Her friends also gave her an elaborate farewell party at which the balance was raised to pay her fare home.

Angelou was astonished with the change in her nine-year-old son when she returned home. When she had left a year before, he was a "loquacious, beautiful and bubbling child." He was now a "rough skinned, shy boy who hung his head when spoken to and refused to maintain eye contact."[43] Angelou found it difficult to pick up where she left off. She couldn't escape the guilt she felt over the traumatizing effect her trip to Europe had had on Clyde. Consumed with guilt, she contemplated suicide but felt that her death would have an even more devastating effect on her son. After ordering him out of the house one day, she telephoned the Langley Porter Psychiatric Clinic to make an appointment to talk to someone about her suicidal feelings. She immediately drove to the clinic.

While speaking with a therapist, Angelou decided that he could not help her because he was white:

Yes, I was troubled; why else would I be here? But what could I tell this man? Would he understand Arkansas, which I left, yet would never, could never, leave? Would he comprehend why my brilliant brother, who was the genius of our family, was doing time in Sing Sing on a charge of fencing stolen goods instead of sitting with clean fingernails in a tailor-made suit, listening to some poor mad person cry her blues out? How would he perceive a mother who had left her only child, who became sick during her absence? A mother who upon her return, felt so guilty she could think of nothing more productive than

killing herself and possibly even the child? No, I couldn't tell him about living inside a skin that was hated or feared by the majority of one's fellow citizens or about the sensation of getting on a bus on a lovely morning, feeling happy and suddenly seeing the passengers curl their lips in distaste or avert their eyes in revulsion. No, I had nothing to say to the doctor.[44]

Angelou took a taxi to her voice coach's studio. After listening to her description of contemplated suicide and despair, he told her to sit down and write what she had to be thankful for. She wrote:

I can hear.
I can speak.
I have a son.
I have a mother.
I have a brother.
I can dance.
I can sing.
I can cook.
I can read.
I can write.[45]

Suddenly she felt silly. She recognized that she was "alive and healthy." At the instruction of her friend, she then wrote: "I am blessed. I am grateful."[46] Angelou left the studio for a theatrical agency, where she applied for work. She returned home with a new lease on life. Soon, Clyde began to blossom again and simultaneously the rash began to disappear. With each day, his fear of her leaving him lessened until he no longer panicked when she left the house without him. One day he announced that he was changing his name to "Guy." After a month, no one could remember calling him anything else.

Chapter

4 Fledgling Writer and Political Activist

The 1950s in the United States were electrified by racial tension and a growing civil rights movement. Blacks mourned the death of fourteen-year-old Emmitt Till, who was found murdered allegedly because he whistled at a white woman. Till's death achieved martyr status when those accused of killing him were freed after a trial. During the 1950s White Citizens' Councils sprang up throughout the South to block school desegregation. Their goal was to indefinitely postpone compliance with the Supreme Court's 1954 *Brown v. Board of Education* decision striking down the separate-but-equal doctrine. In 1955 Rosa Parks was arrested for her refusal to give up her seat to a white passenger on a Montgomery, Alabama, public bus. After a year-long boycott of the bus system by black citizens, the city of Montgomery desegregated city

As the civil rights movement presses on, the first nine students to integrate Little Rock's Central High School are escorted from the school under military guard.

buses. Although Arkansas had made great strides in complying with *Brown,* the governor of Arkansas dispatched troops to prevent nine black students from attending Central High School in Little Rock. In response, President Dwight D. Eisenhower ordered one thousand paratroopers and ten thousand federal troops to escort the nine black children to school and protect them from the angry dissident mobs. In the face of staunch opposition, Congress passed the 1957 Civil Rights Act, which prohibited interfering with a citizen's right to vote.

During this era of violent struggle, Angelou spent several months working at night clubs on the West Coast and Hawaii. After she had saved some money, she moved herself and Guy to a Sausalito, California commune in 1957. In *The Heart of a Woman*, her fourth autobiographical installment, Angelou describes her lifestyle away from America's racial divisiveness:

> I took my young son, Guy, and joined the beatnik brigade. To my mother's dismay, and Guy's great pleasure, we moved across the Golden Gate Bridge and into a house boat commune in Sausalito where I went barefoot, wore jeans, and both of us wore rough-dried clothes. Although I took Guy to a San Francisco barber, I allowed my own hair to grow into a wide unstraightened hedge, which made me look, at a distance, like a tall brown tree whose branches had been clipped. My commune mates, an ichthyologist, a musician, a wife, and an inventor, were white, and had they been political (which they were not), would have occupied a place between the far left and revolution. Strangely, the houseboat offered me

respite from racial tensions and gave my son an opportunity to be around whites who did not think of him as too exotic to need correction, nor so common as to be ignored.[47]

Within a year, Angelou grew tired of the beatnik lifestyle and yearned for "privacy, wall-to-wall carpets and manicures."[48] Furthermore, twelve-year-old Guy was rambunctious and Angelou felt that it was time to return to a more structured lifestyle and more interaction with peers. So she packed up and journeyed to Laurel Canyon, a residential neighborhood of Hollywood where she and Guy settled into a bright two-bedroom bungalow. In 1958, the only blacks who resided in Laurel Canyon were famous jazz artists—Billy Eckstine, Billy Daniels, and Herb Jeffries. The rest of Laurel Canyon's residents were Hollywood's producers, screen stars, and directors. Though she was neither famous nor wealthy, Angelou was attracted to the neighborhood's beauty and glamorous surroundings, and believed that in 1958 Laurel Canyon was the place for an up-and-coming entertainer.

Initially, when Angelou inquired about the bungalow, the landlord told her it was already rented. Angelou then contacted two white friends and asked them to rent the bungalow for her. When they contacted the landlord, he replied that it was available and leased it to them. On the day she moved in, the landlord was cordial and welcomed her white friends. When he noticed Angelou, he realized that he had been tricked into renting to a black woman, shouted obscenities, and threatened to sue, but relented when Angelou's friends told him that they would testify on her behalf.

Angelou painted the house, enrolled Guy in a local school, and purchased a used car. She received a few threatening telephone calls but ignored them. However, several months later, an incident at Guy's school convinced her that she needed to move on. The school contacted Angelou to inform her that Guy would no longer be allowed to ride the school bus because he had used profane language. Angelou determined that Guy had told his white female classmates that babies were conceived when a man and a woman engaged in sexual intercourse and that the girls, learning this for the first time, had cried in response. The school officials proclaimed that they did not allow Negro boys to use foul language when speaking to white girls. Angelou took her son home. Two days later, she received a letter from the school stating that Guy's intelligence qualified him to skip a grade, which would necessitate a change in school when the semester ended. Despite his intelligence, Guy didn't fully apply himself in school, so Angelou concluded the reason for the promotion was not exceptional classroom performance but school officials' desire to expel him from their school.

Angelou decided to move to Westlake, where the residents were ethnically mixed. She rented the second floor of a two-story Victorian and Guy was elated that they now lived in a neighborhood where he was accepted. Except for short out-of-town singing engagements, Angelou and Guy lived in the Westlake District for the next year and a half.

The Harlem Writers Guild

Angelou had previously recorded several songs and lyrics for Liberty Records and now began tinkering with writing prose. Angelou met author John Killens after he came to Hollywood to write the screenplay for his novel *Youngblood.* After reviewing her writing, Killens told her that she had undeniable talent but that her work needed polishing. He told Angelou that she needed to move to New York City where she could benefit from membership and participation in the Harlem Writers Guild, of which he was an active member.

Skyscrapers dominate the skyline of New York City. Angelou moved to the metropolis so that she could join the illustrious Harlem Writers Guild and begin to hone her writing skills.

Angelou had grave reservations about moving again. In the nine years that Guy had been in school, the two had lived in five areas of San Francisco, three areas of Los Angeles, New York City, Hawaii, and Cleveland, Ohio. Consequently, Guy had difficulty making and keeping friends. His reaction to moving to New York City was sullen and resolute. Determined, Angelou decided to journey to New York City ahead of fourteen-year-old Guy and arranged for a friend to stay in their home with him. She sent for him several weeks later after she had found and furnished an apartment.

As planned, Angelou immediately joined the Harlem Writers Guild, which met in John Killens's home. Although the group required no dues and issued no membership cards, participants had to read from their works in progress during their third meeting. In *The Heart of a Woman*, Angelou recalls the humbling experience of reading aloud her one-act play *One Love, One Life:*

> I read the character and set description despite the sudden perversity of my body. The blood pounded in my ears but not enough to drown the skinny sound of my voice. My hands shook so that I had to lay the pages in my lap, but that was not a good solution due to the tricks my knees were playing. They lifted voluntarily, pulling my heels off the floor and then trembled like disturbed Jello. Before I launched into the play's action, I looked around at the writers expecting but hoping not to see their amusement at my predicament. Their faces were studiously blank. Within a year I was to learn each had a horror story about a first reading at the Harlem Writers Guild.[49]

Although the group's criticism of Angelou's writing was brutally honest, their acceptance was genuine as they indicated their desire to hear the next installment of Angelou's play. As Angelou writes in *Heart of a Woman:* "They had stripped me, flayed me, utterly and completely undone me, and now they were as cheery as Christmas cards."[50] After commenting that she looked forward to Angelou's rewrite, writer Paule Marshall forewarned her, "You know, lots of people have more talent than you or I. Hard work makes the difference. Hard, hard unrelenting work."[51] When the evening ended, Angelou promised Killens that she would attend the next meeting. Furthermore, after Killens commented that the short story was the most challenging format, Angelou informed him that her next work would indeed be a short story.

The Apollo Theatre: An End to Singin' and Swingin'

Meanwhile, Angelou found work in a small nightclub on New York's Lower East Side to support herself and Guy. The work embarrassed her. While her friends' artistic works were directed at protesting the systemic racial oppression of blacks, Angelou was merely entertaining people. She quit her job to pursue a more meaningful career, but received an offer she could not refuse, to perform at the famed Apollo Theatre.

Angelou's routine for her Apollo act included an audience-participation song, "Uhuru." Frank Schiffman, the Apollo's manager, didn't believe that the audience would appreciate Angelou's act. Determined, Angelou performed her audience-participation song; despite Schiffman's skepticism, the audience sang along with her and applauded. Word traveled and each night the audience increased in numbers.

The Southern Christian Leadership Conference

Angelou met and befriended actor Godfrey Cambridge at a Greenwich Village party. The two attended a benefit for civil rights leader Reverend Martin Luther King Jr.'s Southern Christian Leadership Conference (SCLC) at a Harlem church. After King's speech, they walked home in silence. Cambridge, the first to speak, declared they must do something to help the cause, and they quickly decided to stage a theater production and donate the proceeds to the SCLC. Angelou met with the New York SCLC's Bayard Rustin, Stanley Levinson, and Jack Murray, who gave their permission and support.

Murray contacted a friend, Art D'Lugoff, who offered the Village Gate, a popular Greenwich Village spot that had hosted acts such as Lenny Bruce, Nina Simone, and Odetta. Angelou and Cambridge assembled actors, singers, dancers, and various technicians, but the proposed play still didn't have a script. Fifteen-year-old Guy had a part-time job in a bakery; each morning when he left for work, Angelou, the designated playwright, was left sitting at a typewriter "constructing plot after unacceptable plot and characters so unreal, they bored even [her]."[52]

Finally, she met with Cambridge and admitted defeat, tearfully confessing that she couldn't write the play. Cambridge suggested that the actors and musicians perform their own skits in the style of the

At a benefit for the Southern Christian Leadership Conference, Martin Luther King Jr.'s forceful words inspired Angelou to join the civil rights movement.

Apollo Theatre and the two named the production *Cabaret for Freedom*. During the summer of 1960 *Cabaret for Freedom* played to sold-out houses which included such notable spectators as actors Sidney Poitier, Ossie Davis, and Ruby Dee, and playwright Lorraine Hansberry.

After *Cabaret for Freedom* closed at the end of the summer, Angelou once again needed employment to support herself and Guy. Desperate for money, Angelou gratefully accepted a two-week singing job in a Chicago nightclub. Before leaving for Chicago, she arranged for someone to come in and cook and clean for fifteen-year-old Guy during her absence. Upon her return, the magazine *Revolución* informed her that it had accepted her short story. She had joined the elite group of writers who were published and the Harlem Writers Guild celebrated.

Impressed with the organizational abilities Angelou displayed during her tenure with *Cabaret for Freedom*, Bayard Rustin and Jack Murray offered her the position of northern coordinator for the SCLC.

Angelou Meets King

Angelou met Martin Luther King Jr. once during her tenure as northern coordinator for the SCLC. She recalls her first impressions of King and their conversation regarding Bailey in The Heart of a Woman.

"I had worked two months for the SCLC, sent out tens of thousands of letters and invitations signed by Rev. King, made hundreds of statements in his name, but I had never seen him up close.

He had an easy friendliness, which was unsettling. Looking at him in my office, alone, was like seeing a lion sitting down at my dining-room table eating a plate of mustard greens. . . . I settled gratefully into the chair and he sat on the arm of the old sofa across the room. . . . When I mentioned my brother Bailey, he asked what he was doing now.

The question stopped me. He was friendly and understanding, but if I told him my brother was in prison, I couldn't be sure how long his understanding would last. I could lose my job. Even more important, I might lose his respect. . . . I took a chance and told him Bailey was in Sing Sing. He dropped his head and looked at his hands.

'It wasn't a crime against a human being.' I had to explain. I loved my brother and although he was in jail, I wanted Martin Luther King to think he was an uncommon criminal. 'He was a fence. Selling stolen goods. That's all.'

He looked up. 'How old is he?' 'Thirty-three and very bright. Bailey is not a bad person. Really.' 'I understand. Disappointment drives our young men to some desperate lengths.' Sympathy and sadness kept his voice low. 'That's why we must fight and win. We must save the Baileys of the world. And Maya, never stop loving him. Never give up on him. Never deny him. And remember, he is freer than those who hold him behind bars.'

Martin Luther King had been a hero and a leader to me since the time when Godfrey and I heard him speak and had been carried to glory on his wings of hope. However, the personal sadness he showed when I spoke of my brother put his heart in my keeping forever, and made me thrust away the small constant worry which my mother had given me as a part of an early parting gift: Black folks can't change because white folks won't change."

Angelou held the position for seven months, during which she coordinated the fund-raising activities for the New York SCLC office and region. These duties included coordinating the volunteer efforts of high school students and soliciting contributions from sympathetic organizations and individuals.

Angelou's days with the SCLC ended when she met South African freedom fighter Vusumzi Make. Make, a member of the Pan-African Congress (PAC), had come to New York with African National Congress (ANC) president Oliver Tambo to raise money for his PAC. Make was taken with Angelou and romantically pursued her. After a few meetings, Angelou and Make agreed to live together. Shortly after their agreement to live as husband and wife, which was not formalized, they journeyed to England, where Make was scheduled to appear at a freedom fighter conference.

A Freedom Fighter's Wife

After honeymooning in London while Make attended a political conference, Angelou returned to New York and rented and furnished a Manhattan apartment. The family lived luxuriously and an affectionate bond grew between Make and Guy. Make visited Guy's school and helped him with his homework during the evenings he was home. Make insisted on a traditional marriage and expected Angelou to spend her time caring for the house. Angelou describes her typical day in *The Heart of a Woman:*

It seemed to me that I washed, scrubbed, mopped, dusted and waxed thoroughly every day. Vus was particu-

lar. He checked on my progress. Sometimes he would pull the sofa away from the wall to see if possibly I had missed a layer of dust. If he found his suspicions confirmed, his response could wither me. He would drop his eyes and shake his head, his face saddened with disappointment. I wiped down the walls, because dirty fingerprints could spoil his day, and ironed his starched shirts (he had his shoes polished professionally).[53]

She continued to attend Monday night Harlem Writers Guild meetings but often dozed, exhausted, during the readings.

Bored with unfulfilling housewife duties and frustrated by her loss of independence, Angelou readily accepted invitations to join a political activist organization and perform in a play. Angelou and other members of the Harlem Writers Guild formed the Cultural Association for Women of African Heritage (CAWAH). The organization's purpose was to "support all black civil rights groups" through producing theatrical benefits and participating in "general protest marches."[54] Following their attendance at a speech by activist Malcolm X, Angelou and five other CAWAH members planned a small demonstration at the general session of the United Nations to protest the assassination of African leader Patrice Lumumba. They expected approximately fifty participants. They were unprepared for the thousands who congregated outside the United Nations building on 125th Street to voice their support. That evening, Angelou and her compatriots watched the media coverage of the demonstration on the evening news. Inspired by the day's events, they agreed to seek guidance for the organization's future involvement in the struggle from Malcolm X.

Militant civil rights activist Malcolm X discounted the passive resistance offered by groups like Angelou's Cultural Association for Women of African Heritage.

Malcolm was supportive but chided the group for its naivete. He patiently expressed his belief that public demonstrations with marchers chanting Christian slogans of equality and injustice could not help end oppression and violence against black leaders. He reasoned that the same Christian concepts had been used to justify slavery and segregation. He concluded that his organization, the Nation of Islam, would not join them in their demonstration, but would support their motives for doing so, unlike other conservative black politicians who charged that the demonstration was irresponsible and not reflective of the black community as a whole.

Unable to survive the backlash of black political conservatives, CAWAH eventually disbanded and Angelou was once again isolated. Make left the house early and returned long after dark. With Guy increas-

ingly engaged in his own teenage pursuits, Angelou spent a great deal of time alone. Finally, she received a call from Max Roach about playing the role of the white queen in the production of Jean Genet's play *The Blacks*. Make initially objected, stating that the wife of a diplomat could not go on stage. However, after meeting with Roach and reading the manuscript, he consented because he believed that *The Blacks* was a great play that could raise social issues in 1960 as he worked to improve the deplorable racial conditions in South Africa and the United States addressed the civil rights movement, now well under way. The off-Broadway play starred Roscoe Lee Browne, Godfrey Cambridge, Cicely Tyson, Louis Gossett Jr., and James Earl Jones. Author James Baldwin and the director, Gene Frankel, were friends and Baldwin visited the set during the daily rehearsals. Baldwin,

Angelou, and Make became friends. After two months, Angelou left the production after a dispute with producers.

At that time, Angelou became aware of the family's deteriorating financial condition when an eviction notice was posted on the door. Alarmed, she notified Make, whose response was to announce that he would take care of things. He returned to the apartment several hours later and informed Angelou and Guy that he had sold the furniture and that a moving truck would come to take their belongings to a hotel, where he had rented a furnished apartment. He offered no explanation for their dire financial straits. After spending three weeks in a musty hotel, Make moved the family to Cairo, Egypt.

In Cairo, Make arranged for the family to occupy a lavishly furnished house in an exclusive neighborhood complete with servants. However, they had only lived there two months when creditors began demanding that Angelou return the furniture and carpets for nonpayment. Twice Guy's school notified his mother that his tuition was in arrears.

Desperate, she sought help from fellow black American David DuBois in finding employment. Through his efforts Angelou was hired as the associate editor for the newspaper *Arab Observer*. She had no journalistic credentials or experience, but Angelou stayed with the *Arab Observer* for over a year. She spent the first two days in the library cramming texts on

---

1960 and *The Blacks*

In a 1977 interview for Encore American & Worldwide News *with Curt Davis, Angelou discusses working with the cast of* The Blacks *and the mood of the country as the civil rights movement gathered momentum.*

"Working for me as a young woman, with the cast of *The Blacks*, was an incredible experience. The original cast included Cecily [sic] Tyson, James Earl Jones, Raymond St. Jacques, Roscoe Lee Browne, Louis Gossett, Charles Gordone, Helen Martin, Cynthia Belgrave, Jay Flash Riley, Lex Monson, Godfrey Cambridge, Ethel Ayler, and me. It was the thing to go into; if you were out of a job, go try out for *The Blacks*. It was wonderful to break down the play together. Obviously it fed all our artistic growth.

In '60–'61 there was an incredible aura—air, is better—of hope. Martin was out there and Malcolm was out there and the Southern Christian Leadership Conference was doing its business. . . . The young people in the country, Black and White, were involved in sit-ins, freedom rides; there was a dream that we could change this country."

A Woman Working in Egypt

Angelou worked as a reporter and associate editor for the Arab Observer *in Cairo for a year. In a 1977 interview with Judith Rich for* Westways, *she recalled the oddity of being the only woman on the staff supervising male reporters and other staff.*

"When I arrived in Cairo I said I wanted to go to work. I just couldn't sit. My husband said that would be utterly impossible; in Egypt nice women didn't work and because of his status I would not be allowed to work. But I had a friend, a black American who was working in a feature news agency. He told me about the *Arab Observer*, the only English news weekly out of the Middle East at the time. He said maybe I'd like to take a chance with that. I got the Africa Desk–Politics. It was really interesting, because I was, at once, a female, non-Muslim, non-Arab, American, black and six feet tall. All I needed was that I should be Jewish! It was a shock to the community. It was really terrifying, that each time I spoke, each time the magazine came out, there was the question of: Was that my point of view, or was I speaking for my husband? But anyway, I lasted. All the other journalists were male and the idea of having a woman even work there, let alone a woman as boss, was ridiculous. But we worked it out and every one worked when I went there."

journalism, writing, Africa, printing, publishing, and editing. Angelou learned how to write opinion articles and the mechanics of layout and editing from her staff members. She also began writing commentaries for Radio Egypt to further supplement her income. During this time Angelou decided to leave Make. In an attempt to persuade her to stay, Make threw her a surprise birthday party that was a disguise for an "African palaver"—a court composed of friends and family convened to determine the couple's future and assign responsibility for the relationship's deterioration. The palaver participants concluded that Make was wrong and that Angelou was justified in her desire to leave him. Nevertheless, at the palaver's request, Angelou agreed to stay six months. Again, her future was uncertain.

5 Defining Home

Unsurprisingly, Angelou and Make were unable to revive their marriage. The couple mutually agreed to end their relationship and parted amicably. In July 1962, Angelou decided to move to Ghana and enroll seventeen-year-old Guy in the University of Ghana. Make provided assistance with airplane tickets and temporary housing in Ghana. Angelou accepted a position with the Liberian Department of Information and planned to settle in Liberia after Guy was settled in the university dormitory in Ghana. However, after they arrived in Ghana, Guy was involved in a serious automobile accident that left him in a full-body cast with a broken neck. Angelou stayed in Ghana with Guy during his four-month recovery, after which he enrolled in the University of Ghana as planned. In the final pages of *The Heart of a Woman*, Angelou recalls the important crossroad in her life:

> Guy was moving into Mensa Sarba Hall. I had seen his room in the dormitory and it looked too small and too dark, but he loved it. For the first time in his life, he was going to live alone, away from my persistent commands. Responsible to himself and for himself. My reaction was in direct contrast to his excitement. I was going to be alone, also, for the first time. I was in my mother's house at his birth, and we had been together ever since. Sometimes we lived with others or they lived with us, but he had always been the powerful axle of my life. . . .
>
> I closed the door and held my breath. Waiting for the wave of emotion to surge over me, knock me down, take my breath away. Nothing happened. I didn't feel bereft or desolate. I didn't feel lonely or abandoned.
>
> I sat down, still waiting. The first thought that came to me, perfectly formed and promising, was "At last, I'll be able to eat the whole breast of roast chicken by myself."[55]

Angelou was enchanted with Ghana and didn't want to leave after Guy's recovery. Other black American immigrants had embraced her. In Africa, the feeling of oppression slowly dissipated. She now lived in a country that was ruled by blacks. Laws were created by blacks and enforced by blacks. She no longer had to fear retaliation from others based on the color of her skin. The black American contingent, led by W. E. B. Du Bois and his wife, Shirley Graham, was composed of four groups: teachers and farmers; American government personnel; businessmen; and the

W. E. B. Du Bois, the renowned American educator, editor, and writer, pioneered the pan-African movement in Ghana.

group to which Angelou considered herself a member, those dedicated to pan-Africanism. Angelou referred to the group as the Revolutionary Returnees. They had answered the call of Ghanian president Kwame Nkrumah, who had publicly welcomed black Americans to Ghana and offered a safe haven to South African revolutionaries and their East African counterparts who were working to end colonialism in their countries.

Contrary to their hopes and expectations, however, the Ghanians' response to the black Americans' arrival ranged from aloof indifference to suspicion and scorn. Ghana's independence from Britain had been won only five years earlier and when an assassination attempt was made on President Nkrumah, the Soviets and then black Americans were the first suspects.

Angelou was gravely disappointed about her displacement in Ghana. She had expected to be embraced by Africans as family. Instead, Africans generally treated black Americans as foreign strangers. Yet she persevered. Angelou openly embraced Ghana's cultural offerings, immediately donning the beautiful flowing fabrics and head wraps and learning the language and customs. She worked as an administrative assistant at the University of Ghana, where she was responsible for maintaining student records and teaching dance and drama. Angelou's pay from the university was enough for rent and Guy's tuition. To earn extra money, she wrote commentaries on American racism for the *Ghanaian Times*.

Angelou shared a bungalow with two other black American women. One evening as they pored over American periodicals, the group discussed Martin Luther King's impending March on Washington, scheduled for August 27, 1963. Despite their consensus that King's nonviolent approach was ineffective, Angelou and her friends decided to stage their own march in front of the American embassy in support of King. Angelou explains her ambivalence in *All God's Children Need Traveling Shoes:*

> My policy was to keep quiet when Reverend King's name was mentioned. I didn't want to remind my radical friends of my association with the peacemaker. It was difficult, but I managed to dispose of the idea that my silence was betrayal. After all, when I worked for him, I had been deluded into agreeing with Reverend King that love would cure America of its pathological illnesses, that indeed our struggle for equal rights would redeem the country's baleful history. But all the

prayers, sit-ins, sacrifices, jail sentences, humiliation, insults and jibes had not borne out Reverend King's vision. When maddened White citizens and elected political leaders vowed to die before they would see segregation come to an end, I became more resolute in rejecting nonviolence and more adamant in denying Martin Luther King.[56]

The march commenced at midnight; as the sun began to peek over the horizon, Angelou realized that the Revolutionary Returnees were the only marchers left:

> Many of us had only begun to realize in Africa that the Stars and Stripes was our flag and our only flag, and that knowledge was almost too painful to bear. We could physically return to Africa, find jobs, learn languages, even marry and remain on African soil all our lives, but we were born in the United States and it was the United

The Story of Keta

Angelou writes in the final pages of All God's Children Need Traveling Shoes *of her journey to the village of Keta. On Angelou's arrival, two older women could not believe that she was not a member of their tribe. Angelou's traveling companion explained that during the slave trade, a few children of the village had escaped as others were taken or killed. The women believed she was a descendant of a native of Keta taken into slavery.*

"The first woman continued leading me from stall to stall, introducing me. Each time the merchant would disbelieve the statement that I was an American Negro, and each time she would gasp and mourn, moan and offer me her goods.

The women wept and I wept. I too cried for the lost people, their ancestors and mine. But I was also weeping with a curious joy. Despite the murders, rapes and suicides, we had survived. The middle passage and the auction block had not erased us. Not humiliations nor lynchings, individual cruelties nor collective oppression had been able to eradicate us from the earth. We had come through despite our own ignorance and gullibility, and the ignorance and rapacious greed of our assailants.

There was much to cry for, much to mourn, but in my heart, I felt exalted knowing there was much to celebrate. Although separated from our languages, our families and customs, we had dared to continue to live. We had crossed the unknowable oceans in chains and had written its mystery into 'Deep River, my home is over Jordan.' Through the centuries of despair and dislocation, we had been creative, because we faced down death by daring to hope."

States which had rejected, enslaved, exploited and denied us. It was the United States which held the graves of our grandmothers and grandfathers. It was in the United States, under conditions too bizarre to detail, that those same ancestors had worked and dreamed of "a better day, by and by."[57]

Tired and disillusioned, Angelou writes that she "went home alone, emptied of passion and too exhausted to cry."[58]

In 1964 Angelou again met Malcolm X when he visited Ghana after severing his ties with the segregationist Nation of Islam. In Egypt, he had learned that the true spirit of Allah demanded that he and other Islamic worshipers embrace all who worshiped Allah regardless of skin color or race.

Although her work kept her busy and she had an active and fulfilling social life, Angelou writes that "Ghana was beginning to tug at me and make me uncomfortable, like an ill fitting coat."[59] She played the lead in Bertolt Brecht's *Mother Courage,* yet, she felt that she was not in her right place. After some thought, she admitted to herself that the rift between her and nineteen-year-old Guy over his relationship with a woman older than Angelou was the driving force behind her need to get out of Africa. When she approached Guy about the relationship, he insisted that he must lead his own life. Instead of angering Guy by speaking to the woman, Angelou decided that she needed to distance herself from Guy.

She quickly accepted Sidney Bernstein's invitation to perform in the Berlin and Venice tour of Genet's *The Blacks.* The

A Ghanian woman travels to a local marketplace with a large bundle of corn balanced on her head. While in Ghana, Angelou budded as an aspiring civil rights activist and writer, but she could never consider the country her home.

Martin Luther King Jr. (center) gives a speech during a civil rights rally in Atlanta. As Angelou became engrossed in the civil rights movement, she began to distance herself from King and his nonviolent approach.

tour was a success and Angelou enjoyed a rcunion with old friends Cicely Tyson, Louis Gossett Jr., and particularly Roscoe Lee Browne.

Angelou left Venice and joined other Revolutionary Returnees in Cairo for a political conference. Angelou concluded her stay in Cairo by attending a formal dinner where she was also scheduled to sing with William V. S. Tubman, Egypt's president. Tubman and his officials were delighted with her rendition of "Swing Low, Sweet Chariot" and joined her in singing other Negro spirituals.

Upon her return to Ghana, she sensed that in her absence she and Guy had re-paired their rift. However, she was unprepared for the coming-of-age speech he delivered before she could change from her traveling clothes. He complimented her on how she had raised him and then informed her that he was now a man with his own life, just as she had her own life.

Disappointed with Africa and realizing that Guy did not need her, Angelou took advantage of an opportunity Malcolm X had told her about, the need for experienced coordinators by the Organization for Afro-American Unity, or OAAU. Angelou decided to return and lend the skills she had polished working for King's Southern Christian Leadership Conference. In *All*

God's Children Need Traveling Shoes, Angelou rationalizes her return to the United States:

> It seemed that I had gotten all Africa had to give me. . . . I had seen the African moon grow red as fire over the black hills at Aburi and listened to African priests implore God in rhythm and voices which carried me back to Calvary Baptist Church in San Francisco.
>
> If the heart of Africa still remained elusive, my search for it had brought me closer to understanding myself and other human beings. The ache for home lives in all of us, the safe place where we can go as we are and not be questioned. It impels mighty ambitions and dangerous capers. We amass great fortunes at the cost of our souls, or risk our lives in drug dens from London's Soho, to San Francisco's Haight-Ashbury. We shout in Baptist churches, wear yarmulkes and wigs and argue even the tiniest points in the Torah, or worship the sun and refuse to kill cows for the starving. Hoping that by doing these things home will find us acceptable or failing that, that we will forget our awful yearning for it.
>
> My mind was made up. I would go back to the United States as soon as possible.[60]

Her friends were sorry to see her leave but when she told Guy, he smiled broadly and agreed that it was time for her to return home. She told him that she had paid his tuition and opened a bank account in his name. He thanked her for the money and promised that he would try to become financially independent as soon as possible.

Angelou arrived in the United States on February 19, 1965. Malcolm X was assassinated in New York City two days later. In an interview with Stephanie Caruana, Angelou discusses the impact of Malcolm's death:

> After that, I decided to have nothing to do with politics directly. I wrote a play, then wrote and produced a television series in San Francisco. Then I went to Algiers, and to Senegal. I haven't dared

During a 1964 visit to Ghana, civil rights leader Malcolm X encouraged Angelou to return to the United States and help coordinate the fledgling Organization for Afro-American Unity.

New York City police officers carry the body of slain hero Malcolm X away from the scene of his barbarous assassination on February 21, 1965. Following Malcolm's death, Angelou would abandon politics.

go back to Ghana because my experience there was so precious that I don't want to risk spoiling it. I got so much health and stability from that country and the people, the way it was with Kwame Nkrumah. He was deposed and subsequently killed and I haven't wanted to go back.[61]

Angelou accepted a lecturer position with the University of California at Los Angeles and began focusing on writing short stories, poems, song lyrics, and dramas. Her two-act play *The Least of These* was produced in Los Angeles and Angelou later wrote and produced a brief television series for a San Francisco station. Later she authored another two-act drama, *The Clawing Within*, and a two-act musical, *Adjoa Amissah*. In 1968 Angelou narrated a ten-part television series about African traditions in American life for public television and in 1969 she recorded an album of her work, *The Poetry of Maya Angelou.*

Chapter

6 The Works of a Mature Artist

The 1970s and 1980s were powerhouse decades for Angelou. Angelou's first autobiography, *I Know Why the Caged Bird Sings*, published in 1970, received critical acclaim and won her worldwide recognition. *Caged Bird* was the first book authored by a black woman to climb the *New York Times* best-seller list and was nominated for a National Book Award. Author James Baldwin praised the work in a critical essay:

> [*Caged Bird*] liberates the reader into life simply because Maya Angelou confronts her own life with such a moving wonder, such a luminous dignity. I have no words for this achievement; but I know that not since the days of my childhood, when the people in books were more real than the people one saw every day, have I found myself so moved. . . . Her portrait is a biblical study of life in the midst of death.[62]

In an interview with Judith Rich, Angelou describes how her inability to ignore a challenge contributed to the birth of *Caged Bird*:

> I really got roped into writing *The Caged Bird*. At that time, I was really only concerned with poetry, though I'd written a television series. Anyway, James Baldwin took me to a party at Jules Feiffer's house. It was just the four of us: Jimmy Baldwin and me, Jules Feiffer and his wife, at that time Judy Feiffer. We sat up until three or four o'clock in the morning, drinking scotch and telling tales. The next morning Judy Feiffer called a friend at Random House and said, "You know the poet, Maya Angelou? If you can get her to write a book. . . ." Then Robert Loomis at Random House phoned, and I said, "No, I'm not interested. Thank you so much." Then, I'm sure he talked to Baldwin because he used a ploy which I'm not proud to say I haven't gained control of yet. He called and said, "Miss Angelou it's been nice talking to you. I'm rather glad you decided not to write an autobiography because to write an autobiography, as literature, is the most difficult thing anyone can do." I said, "I'll do it." Now that's an area I don't have control of yet at this age. The minute someone says I can't, all my energy goes up and I say, what? What? I'm still unable to say that you may be wrong and walk away. I'm not pleased with that. I want to get beyond that.[63]

Angelou didn't stop to bask in her almost instantaneous fame with the public acceptance of *Caged Bird*. She continued to work at a frenzied pace and accepted the appointment of poet in residence at the University of Kansas. In 1971 Angelou published *Just Give Me a Cool Drink of Water 'Fore I Diiie*, a collection of poetry that includes selections from her 1969 recording and was nominated for a Pulitzer Prize. Angelou became the first black woman to have an original script produced when Independent-Cinerama filmed her screenplay *Georgia, Georgia* in 1972. Angelou also composed the score for the movie. Diana Sands starred in Angelou's film, which explores the complexities of interracial relationships and what Angelou perceived as the rift between black men and women. *Georgia, Georgia* was filmed in Sweden and Angelou later returned there to study cinematography.

In 1973 Angelou played Mary Todd Lincoln's dressmaker in the Broadway play *Look Away* and won a Tony nomination for her efforts. She also married builder Paul De Feu. Basking in the happiness generated by her new marriage, Angelou and her new husband settled in a tranquil retreat in the Sonoma Valley of northern California. Angelou enjoyed the seclusion and familiarity with people and local politics that small-town life offered. Meanwhile, often accompanied by Paul, she busied herself with lecture tours, writing, and her budding dramatic efforts.

Angelou devoted most of 1974 to writing her screenplay *All Day Long*. She also taught English, literature, and philosophy as a visiting professor at Wake Forest University, Wichita State University, and California State University at Sacramento. Random House, Angelou's publisher, released her second autobiographical work, *Gather Together in My Name*, and her adaptation of Sophocles' *Ajax*. Even with plans to

Angelou's career skyrocketed following the 1970 publication of I Know Why the Caged Bird Sings. *She achieved notoriety not only for her writing and acting endeavors but also for her forceful lectures.*

teach at Sacramento State University the following year and a Bill Moyers television special in the works, Angelou, a renowned cook, looked forward to clearing some of the Sonoma property to plant a vegetable garden. Although she and Paul traveled extensively, the down-to-earth Angelou insisted on quiet evening meals at home that often included close friends and family.

Angelou and De Feu capped off 1975 by spending November and December at the famed Rockefeller Foundation Bellagio Study Center in Italy, where Angelou was one of fifteen international scholars in residence. During that year Angelou released another volume of poetry, *Oh Pray My Wings Are Gonna Fit Me Well*, received honorary degrees from Smith College and

Mills College, finished her work on President Gerald Ford's Bicentennial Commission, was appointed to the board of trustees of the American Film Institute, and recorded *An Evening with Maya Angelou* for Pacific Tape Library.

In 1976 she continued her dramatic efforts with the production of her play *And Still I Rise*. Angelou directed the play's performance at the Ensemble Theater in Oakland, California. *Singin' and Swingin' and Gettin' Merry like Christmas*, her third autobiographical work, was published and she and Paul embarked on a nationwide lecture and book promotion tour.

Desiring very much to be taken seriously in film, Angelou continued to act and direct. She directed two National Educational Television films, which were aired in November 1976. In 1977 she received an Emmy nomination for her portrayal of Nyo Boto in Alex Haley's miniseries *Roots*. Of course, while developing her film and dramatic talents, she continued to write. In 1978, she released her third collection of poetry, *And Still I Rise*.

Maya the Educator

Following the publication of her fourth autobiographical installment, *The Heart of a Woman*, in 1981 and her divorce from Paul De Feu, Angelou accepted Wake Forest University's lifetime appointment as the Z. Smith Reynolds Professor of American Studies. She teaches one semester a year, which permits her to continue her writing, dramatic, and film pursuits. She published two more volumes of poetry, *Shaker, Why Don't You Sing?* (1983) and *Now Sheba Sings the Song* (1987) in collaboration with Tom Feelings. In 1986 she published her fifth autobiographical work, *All God's Children Need Traveling Shoes*.

During a tribute sponsored by the Center for Democratic Renewal, a national clearinghouse for hate crimes information, an emotional Angelou is honored for her many accomplishments.

A Day in the Life of Maya Angelou

The following article by Carol Sarler appeared in the December 27, 1987, issue of the Sunday Times Magazine.

"I wake usually about six and get immediately out of bed. I make very strong coffee and sit in the sunroom with the newspaper. . . .

At about 8:30 I start looking at the house because the housekeeper arrives at nine and I'm still too well brought-up to offer Mrs. Cunningham a house in too much disarray. . . . She has been my housekeeper for six years now. I give to her and she gives to me and we live together with a lot of laughter. My secretary, Mrs. Garris, also comes at nine and that's when real life begins.

At ten I deal with my correspondence; I get about 300 letters a week. I'm a very serious cook and I prepare what to me is a fabulous lunch for two or three people. . . .

In the afternoon I read—if I'm teaching I read works coming out of the theme of my class and I put on the music to complement the reading. For instance, if I'm doing a course on African culture's impact on the world I will read *Basil Davidson's Last Kingdoms of Africa* and I'll put on tapes of African music . . . and I turn it up very loud, it's all over my house, that insistence of the music which helps to entrench me into the era. Unless I'm involved in something really important, Mrs. Garris and Mrs. Cunningham come up to say goodbye at five. . . .

At the time I suppose it's tea-time for other people, I help myself to a very nice drink—Dewar's White Label whiskey—and I look at my paintings. . . .

About seven I start to prepare dinner for myself; I drink more than I eat, but I prepare a proper dinner and put on candles and pretty music—all for me. If I'm not good to myself, how can I expect anyone else to be good to me? Then I read again, unless there's something on the television. . . .

If I do go out I like to go to friends—however, unless there is an issue which calls for immediate discussion, I don't like cocktail chit-chat over Israel, or the Arabs. I think everyone young should do that with lots of cheap wine, sitting on the floor and shouting and arguing, but I don't do it now."

Angelou continues to challenge and inspire new generations as a professor of black literature and cultural history at Wake Forest University.

Angelou teaches black literature and cultural history, the underpinning of both of which is her belief that the greatest teachers inspire their students to desire knowledge. Commenting on Angelou's student reception at Wake Forest, dean of students Thomas Mullen stated:

> She had the audience so caught up that by the end of the evening they were standing up and firing questions at her right and left. . . . Usually you have to pry questions out of kids. She opened them up. She made them feel something.[64]

Her goal in teaching is the same as her goal as a writer or friend: "My aspiration is not achievable, which may be all right if I accept that the process is more important than the result. . . . I want to know more—not intellectually—to know more so I can be a better human being, to be an honest, courageous, funny and loving human being. That's what I want to be—and I blow it about 86 times a day. My hope is to cut that to 70."[65]

The Writing Process

The themes of responsibility, humanity, and survival are central to everything Angelou does. Angelou is emphatic that her responsibility as a writer is to be as good as she can be at her craft:

> Its not just a matter of letting it all hang out. . . . Learning the craft, understanding what language can do, gaining control of language, enables one to make one weep, make them laugh, even make them go to war. You can do this by learning how to harness the power of the word.[66]

Essential to Angelou's theme of survival is survival with *style*. She believes that as an artist, the ability to take risks is important:

> I believe that probably the most important single thing, beyond discipline, in any artistic work is to *dare*. To write, I have to feel as if I am in some uninhabitable place with some people, and everybody else has come out but they're afraid. And I dare to go out and test the ledge. Then, after that, I can dare a little bit more. I can dare to just sort of get over and hang on. The person who dares to go out there and test the ledge, that shaky place: that's the artist.[67]

Angelou cautions that daring to try does not necessarily mean succeeding:

> Now, not everything you do is going to be a masterpiece. But it's only in certain societies where everything you do has to be perfect. But you get out there and you really try and sometimes you really do, you write that masterpiece, you sing that classic. The other times

you're just stretching your soul, you're stretching your instrument, your mind. That's good.[68]

A New Chapter

At age seventy-one, Angelou remains a productive artist. Her 1993 collection of inspirational essays and life lessons, *Wouldn't Give Nothing for My Journey Now*, is dedicated to good friend, fellow filmmaker and popular talk show host Oprah Winfrey. In 1997 she published her second volume of essays, *Even the Stars Look Lonesome*, in which she pays tribute to her mother, who died in 1992, before she could see her daughter in her role as inaugural poet. The collection of essays also explores Angelou's life lessons on love and marriage, aging, the necessity of art, and the joy that a home can give.

As her books continued to grace the best-seller lists, Angelou spent the summer of 1998 directing the Miramax feature film *Down in the Delta*. Released on Christmas Day 1998, the film stars Alfre Woodard, Wesley Snipes, Esther Rolle, Al Freeman Jr., Mary Alice, and Loretta Devine. Angelou states that the "film is about family breaking up and coming back together. I was really caught that this young man [author Myron Goble] had written a story about a black family which could have been told

An aging Maya Angelou poses for a portrait in her home. The amazing artist has not let her years slow her down; she continues to produce moving poetry and literature and forges ahead in the film industry.

about an Irish family, or a Jewish family. It could have been done in Canton, Ohio and Canton, China."[69]

Despite her prolific successes, Angelou considers her golden years the most difficult: "What's really hard about getting older is not the thickening of the waist or the cracking of the hips and knees, it's the absence of the beloveds. Some people who start with you go on before you to their other destinations."[70] She singles out the differences in visits to New York since the deaths of friends Betty Shabazz and Jessica Mitford.

Yet Angelou, a self-described workaholic, continues to write, her greatest joy, and seeks to blaze new trails in the film industry. Her son, Guy, is her "monument, joy, and sheer delight."[71] Looking forward to the December 1998 release of Guy's first book, *Standing at the Scratch Line*, with exuberant pride, Angelou states:

My son turned out to be magnificent. But then I learned about mothering from my own mother. And Guy says he learned how to raise his stepson from me. This works with family—it even works with my actors. Hands off. Just tell someone you love them all the time and leave them alone.[72]

Notes

Introduction: Maya Angelou: America's Spiritual Adviser

1. Quoted in Jeffrey M. Elliot, ed., *Conversations with Maya Angelou.* Jackson: University Press of Mississippi, 1989, p. 96.

2. Quoted in Elliot, *Conversations with Maya Angelou*, p. 94.

3. Quoted in Elliot, *Conversations with Maya Angelou*, pp. 142–43.

4. Quoted in Elliot, *Conversations with Maya Angelou*, p. 152.

Chapter 1: Growing Up Black, Southern, and Female

5. Maya Angelou, *Gather Together in My Name.* New York: Random House, 1974, p. 76.

6. Maya Angelou, *I Know Why the Caged Bird Sings.* New York: Random House, 1970, pp. 2–4.

7. Angelou, *I Know Why the Caged Bird Sings*, pp. 4, 272.

8. Angelou, *I Know Why the Caged Bird Sings*, p. 23.

9. Angelou, *I Know Why the Caged Bird Sings*, p. 57.

10. Angelou, *I Know Why the Caged Bird Sings*, pp. 47–48.

11. Angelou, *I Know Why the Caged Bird Sings*, p. 79.

12. Angelou, *I Know Why the Caged Bird Sings*, p. 94.

13. Angelou, *I Know Why the Caged Bird Sings*, pp. 98, 101.

14. Angelou, *I Know Why the Caged Bird Sings*, p. 170.

15. Quoted in Angelou, *I Know Why the Caged Bird Sings*, p. 197.

16. Angelou, *I Know Why the Caged Bird Sings*, p. 215.

17. Angelou, *I Know Why the Caged Bird Sings*, p. 215.

18. Angelou, *I Know Why the Caged Bird Sings*, p. 254.

19. Angelou, *I Know Why the Caged Bird Sings*, p. 274.

Chapter 2: Teenage Motherhood and Making a Living

20. Angelou, *Gather Together in My Name*, pp. 3–4.

21. Angelou, *Gather Together in My Name*, p. 31.

22. Angelou, *Gather Together in My Name*, p. 33.

23. Angelou, *Gather Together in My Name*, p. 36.

24. Angelou, *Gather Together in My Name*, pp. 36–37.

25. Angelou, *Gather Together in My Name*, p. 44.

26. Angelou, *Gather Together in My Name*, p. 70.

27. Angelou, *Gather Together in My Name*, p. 118.

28. Angelou, *Gather Together in My Name*, p. 195.

29. Angelou, *Gather Together in My Name*, p. 207.

30. Angelou, *Gather Together in My Name*, pp. 214–15.

31. Angelou, *Gather Together in My Name*, p. 215.

Chapter 3: Married Life and the Making of a Performer

32. Maya Angelou, *Singin' and Swingin' and Gettin' Merry like Christmas.* New York: Random House, 1976, pp. 12–13.

33. Quoted in Elliot, *Conversations with Maya Angelou*, p. 30.

34. Angelou, *Singin' and Swingin' and Gettin' Merry like Christmas*, p. 14.

35. Angelou, *Singin' and Swingin' and Gettin' Merry like Christmas*, p. 15.

36. Angelou, *Singin' and Swingin' and Gettin' Merry like Christmas*, p. 17.

37. Angelou, *Singin' and Swingin' and Gettin' Merry like Christmas*, p. 27.

38. Angelou, *Singin' and Swingin' and Gettin' Merry like Christmas*, p. 28.

39. Angelou, *Singin' and Swingin' and Gettin' Merry like Christmas*, pp. 29–30.

40. Angelou, *Singin' and Swingin' and Gettin' Merry like Christmas*, p. 30.

41. Angelou, *Singin' and Swingin' and Gettin' Merry like Christmas*, pp. 31–32.

42. Angelou, *Singin' and Swingin' and Gettin' Merry like Christmas*, p. 127.

43. Angelou, *Singin' and Swingin' and Gettin' Merry like Christmas*, p. 257.

44. Angelou, *Singin' and Swingin' and Gettin' Merry like Christmas*, p. 260.

45. Angelou, *Singin' and Swingin' and Gettin' Merry like Christmas*, p. 262.

46. Angelou, *Singin' and Swingin' and Gettin' Merry like Christmas*, p. 262.

Chapter 4: Fledgling Writer and Political Activist

47. Maya Angelou, *The Heart of a Woman*. New York: Random House, 1981, p. 2.

48. Angelou, *The Heart of a Woman*, p. 2.

49. Angelou, *The Heart of a Woman*, p. 42.

50. Angelou, *The Heart of a Woman*, p. 45.

51. Quoted in Angelou, *The Heart of a Woman*, p. 48.

52. Angelou, *The Heart of a Woman*, p. 72.

53. Angelou, *The Heart of a Woman*, p. 166.

54. Angelou, *The Heart of a Woman*, p. 169.

Chapter 5: Defining Home

55. Angelou, *The Heart of a Woman*, pp. 323–24.

56. Maya Angelou, *All God's Children Need Traveling Shoes*. New York: Random House, 1986, pp. 121–22.

57. Angelou, *All God's Children Need Traveling Shoes*, p. 127.

58. Angelou, *All God's Children Need Traveling Shoes*, p. 128.

59. Angelou, *All God's Children Need Traveling Shoes*, p. 147.

60. Angelou, *All God's Children Need Traveling Shoes*, p. 195.

61. Quoted in Elliot, *Conversations with Maya Angelou*, p. 33.

Chapter 6: The Works of a Mature Artist

62. Quoted in Mary E. Williams, ed., *Readings on Maya Angelou*. San Diego: Greenhaven Press, 1997, p. 26.

63. Quoted in Elliot, *Conversations with Maya Angelou*, p. 151.

64. Quoted in Elliot, *Conversations with Maya Angelou*, pp. 171–72.

65. Quoted in Elliot, *Conversations with Maya Angelou*, p. 211.

66. Quoted in Elliot, *Conversations with Maya Angelou*, p. 149.

67. Quoted in Elliot, *Conversations with Maya Angelou*, p. 16.

68. Quoted in Elliot, *Conversations with Maya Angelou*, p. 51.

69. Quoted in Nadine Brozan, "Chronicle: Maya Angelou Shifts Gears," *New York Times*, August 25, 1997.

70. Quoted in Dana Kennedy, "Holiday Films: A Poet at 70 Ventures into the Unknown," *New York Times*, November 15, 1998.

71. Quoted in Elliot, *Conversations with Maya Angelou*, p. 203.

72. Quoted in Kennedy, "Holiday Films."

For Further Reading

Books About Maya Angelou

Mary E. Williams, ed., *Readings on Maya Angelou*. San Diego: Greenhaven Press, 1997. A collection of interviews with Angelou and essays regarding the themes that are interwoven throughout her autobiographical works and poetry.

Books by Angelou

Maya Angelou, *Wouldn't Take Nothing for My Journey Now*. New York: Random House, 1993. A collection of inspirational and instructional essays.

————, *Even the Stars Look Lonesome*. New York: Random House, 1997. Angelou's second volume of inspirational essays and life lessons.

Works Consulted

Maya Angelou, *I Know Why the Caged Bird Sings*. New York: Random House, 1970. Angelou's first autobiography details, in fictionalized form, her childhood until age seventeen and the birth of her son.

————, *Gather Together in My Name*. New York: Random House, 1974. Angelou's second autobiographical work details her struggle to maintain employment during the first three years of her son's life.

————, *Singin' and Swingin' and Gettin' Merry like Christmas*. New York: Random House, 1976. The third installment of Angelou's autobiography chronicles her early performance years.

————, *The Heart of a Woman*. New York: Random House, 1981. Angelou's coming-of-age autobiographical work discusses her involvement with civil rights leaders and organizations, and initial writing projects.

————, *All God's Children Need Traveling Shoes*. New York: Random House, 1986. The most recent of Angelou's autobiographical works chronicles her five years in Ghana and involvement with such historical figures as W. E. B. Du Bois and Malcolm X.

Howard G. Chua-Eoan and Nina Burleigh, "Moment of Creation," *People*, January 18, 1993. Discusses Angelou's process for creating the inaugural poem.

Karima A. Haynes, "Maya Angelou: Prime-Time Poet," *Ebony*, April 1993. Interview with Angelou and discussion of her inaugural poem and its aftermath.

Bell Hooks, "There's No Place to Go but Up," *Shambhala Sun*, January 1998. A conversation between poet and author Hooks and Angelou discussing the importance of art, American race relations, and writing.

"Million Man March Draws More than 1 Million Black Men to Nation's Capital," *Jet*, November 1995. Mentions Angelou's appearance as a speaker and the poem she composed in honor of the march.

Index

Picture Credits

About the Author

Terrasita Cuffie is an attorney who focuses primarily on family law and mediation. *The Importance of Maya Angelou* is her first book. She lives in St. Louis, Missouri.